LONG-TERM
GREEDY

LONG-TERM GREEDY

The Triumph of Goldman Sachs

Nils Lindskoog

McCrossen Publishing

LONG-TERM GREEDY:
The Triumph of Goldman Sachs

Copyright © 1998 by Nils Lindskoog
All rights reserved.

Except in the case of brief quotations embodied in critical articles and reviews, no part of this book may be used or reproduced in any manner whatsoever without written permission from the publisher. For information, address McCrossen Publishing, P.O. Box 2132, Appleton, WI 54913.

Library of Congress Catalog Card Number 96-76405

ISBN 0-9652153-3-4

Printed in the United States of America

First Edition

*In memory of the 1980s
and Mom & Dad*

Contents

Introduction	9

PART I. THE DILEMMA

1. The Legacy	15
2. A Tree Grows on Broad Street	24
3. The Milken Arriveth	31
4. Take My Paper, Please!	45

PART II. THE ANSWER

5. The Public LBO	57
6. Goldman Saki	75
7. The Bridge Game	83
8. Barney Kroger's Grocery Wagon	94
9. Crash and Burn	103

PART III. REDEMPTION

10. You Can Go Home Again	115

About the Author	121
Acknowledgements	121
Notes and References	123
Index	155

Introduction

This is an analysis of a previously unexamined aspect of the 1980s and ensuing financial events. The 1980s was the age of leverage, the most creative, destructive, and fascinating period in American financial history. The junk-bond tool popularized by Michael Milken empowered a group of innovators, creating a world of leveraged buyouts and hostile-takeover bids. The consequence of Milken's system was a major disruption of the Wall Street order. Clients and business were swept away from the leading investment-banking firms, which found themselves at a critical disadvantage in trying to compete in the most lucrative game ever.

During the financial revolution that ensued, huge money was made and huge money was lost. Ironically, as fast as the leverage craze came, it was gone. By decade's end, leveraged takeovers had disappeared, Drexel Burnham Lambert was bankrupt, Milken would soon be in prison, LBO funds were cashing out their holdings, and many commercial banks and investment-banking firms were saddled with hangovers brought on by the leverage binge. The sudden demise of the era and wreckage of several of the key players raises the obvious questions: Who profited in the end? Who survived and prospered? Quite simply, *Who won?*

What follows is an account of the means by which one Wall Street firm endured this period. This was a firm that came out of the 1980s a winner—stronger and even more commanding than when the decade began. It was, in fact, one of the firms initially most harmed by leverage, one that had achieved a short-lived dominance that was usurped by the financial innovators and their junk-bond revolution. However, by reshaping the leverage game to fit its own strengths, Goldman Sachs was able to withstand the challenge—and emerged from this period as the most powerful investment-banking firm.

I possessed an interesting vantage point from which to witness and evaluate the events of this era. During the 1980s and early 1990s, I had the privilege of working in the field of mergers and acquisitions, the realm that financial professionals warred over and the discipline that defined the period. I also had the duty of monitoring the takeover vulnerability of a large industrial firm, a company that ultimately took on a leveraged defense advised by Goldman.

My duties thus provided a front-row view of the gamut of methods and ideas of the investment-banking community. Thankfully, however, it was the activities of Goldman Sachs personnel that I was closest to, for theirs were by far the most fascinating.

It is not the purpose of this book to in any way pass judgement on Goldman Sachs or its people. One function of the book, certainly, is to inform the reader of some of the factors in the success of this incredibly successful firm. Another purpose is to educate on the subject of leverage. By understanding the reasons behind the 1980s craze and the factors common to all such episodes, the reader will be prepared to recognize (and avoid) the excesses of these euphorias. The book is also intended to provide a better understanding of specific financial instruments and techniques, especially in regard to corporate acquisitions—thereby helping to reduce the confusion that often arises from such methods.

The account is presented in three parts. Part I, "The Dilemma," supplies background, explaining how the effects of junk bonds created a threat to the clients and business of Goldman Sachs. Part II, "The Solution," describes the development and perfection of a leverage technique utilized by Goldman clients in the 1980s—the "leveraged recapitalization." Part III is "Redemption," where it is shown why Goldman was the firm best positioned to prosper in the aftermath of the leverage era.

By the end of 1991, Goldman Sachs stood atop the financial world. While others licked their 1980s wounds, the last major investment-banking partnership reigned as the king of Wall Street, a firm ready to take advantage of all new opportunities, a firm of fewer than 150 general partners sharing in more than $1 billion in annual profits. Although its role in the decade of debt was not readily evident, ultimately no firm came out of this period better than Goldman Sachs. The reasons for its success will now become apparent.

Part I.
THE DILEMMA

1. The Legacy

There might never have been a Goldman Sachs if Marcus Goldman's wife hadn't suffered a bout of loneliness.

Goldman arrived in America in 1848 from Germany and soon founded a successful clothing store in Philadelphia. Shortly after the Civil War, he had accumulated enough wealth to retire. However, his wife, wishing to be with her friends in New York, encouraged him to move. In 1869, Goldman—in the same manner as merchants-turned-financiers Abraham Kuhn, Solomon Loeb, Joseph Seligman, and the Lehmans—started a business in New York City.

Marcus Goldman's new trade provided a service to merchants in the city. The small-business owners of New York had constant financing needs, but they didn't have time to arrange bank loans. So Goldman would purchase the promissory notes of retailers, then sell the notes to local banks at a profit. From this middleman service of men like Goldman, the commercial-paper business was born.

After Goldman's son-in-law Samuel Sachs entered the firm in 1882, it became Goldman Sachs & Company. For several years the partnership remained a small-time, family house dealing in commercial paper and other financial services. However, when corporate securities started to become more widely accepted in the early 1900s, Goldman (hereafter, "Goldman" will refer to the firm of Goldman Sachs unless otherwise noted) sought to become a competitor in the activity that came to define the profession known as "investment banking"—that activity being the underwriting of securities.

Securities underwriting is a simple concept. When a company wishes to raise money through debt or equity financing, it would have a difficult time marketing an issue on its own. An investment banker "underwrites" a securities offering by in essence saying to the company, "I'll buy all of your issue at an agreed-upon price, write you a check for the negotiated amount (minus a fee, of course), market the securities, and bear the risk of any price fluctuations." The investment banker thus performs an insurance function by taking on the risk of price changes as the securities are sold.

Marcus Goldman's son Henry aspired to get into the underwriting of equity securities (i.e., stocks). Unfortunately, the most popular securities of the early 1900s were of mighty railroads and utilities, and the underwriting of such issues was handled by experienced firms.

Yet Henry Goldman saw much greater potential in equity underwriting. Instead of underwriting just the issues of large entities such as railroads and utilities, he envisioned selling equity securities for his merchant clients. In fact, why couldn't all types and sizes of firms sell stock?

The issue remained whether anyone would accept such securities. To answer this question, Goldman needed a client who required a substantial amount of financing and would employ an unproven firm.

Thanks to a stroke of luck, a blockbuster underwriting deal came to Goldman's doorstep. Years earlier, Samuel Sachs's family had taken in one of their relatives as a boarder. The grateful house-guest was Julius Rosenwald, who had gone on to become president of a growing

Midwest mail-order firm by the name of Sears Roebuck. The Rosenwald connection allowed Goldman to make the first public stock offering of capital-hungry Sears—a $10 million issue in 1906 that was a huge deal by the standards of the day.

Goldman needed help in underwriting and selling such a large offering. To efficiently handle the Sears issue, the assistance of Lehman Brothers and other firms was enlisted. By having several firms purchase the stock and perform a portion of the distribution, the underwriting risk was dispersed—such technique being known as syndication.

The Sears deal was a winner and luckily just beat the Wall Street Panic of 1907. The ensuing recession dampened the securities market for a while, but Goldman soon continued its underwriting activities in earnest. By 1924 the firm had been involved in more than 140 securities issues.*

In the mid-1920s, publicly traded securities took off, as an economic boom and the first mass appearance of disposable income caused rampant financial speculation. Businessmen were anxious to sell stock in their firms after seeing colleagues get rich on shares that had been offered to the public.

The underwriting firms of the day were eager to capitalize on this opportunity. However, to be a truly dominating underwriter, one would have to change the way the game was played. To really cash in on this activity, one needed to create a guaranteed system of securities demand and distribution. The loose structure of the financial markets and modest regulation of the time provided just that opportunity, but it took a certain ingenuity to create a comprehensive system. And in the 1920s, a little financial ingenuity went a long way.

This was also the dawn of a period that repeats every forty to sixty years; that is, the financial markets were succumbing to the lure of

---

*In practice, the term *publicly traded* has come to be limited to securities registered with the Securities and Exchange Commission, which was not created until 1934. However, publicly traded will be used here in reference to pre-1934 securities that were widely held and actively traded.

leverage. With the Panic of 1907 fading from memory and credit becoming easy, the latest fascination with debt was gathering momentum.

To this point, Goldman Sachs had been a relatively prosperous investment-banking house. But given the current speculative fever and embracement of leverage, the partnership had the chance to greatly expand its influence. Goldman Sachs soon perfected an ingenious leverage design. To understand the nature of this system, one must return to the pre-SEC (Securities and Exchange Commission) world of investment banking.

To begin the design, one needed control over a pool of funds. The easiest way to get it was from the public; one simply created one's own publicly traded equity security. The mechanism was a type of mutual fund.

In 1928 Goldman launched its own mutual fund, the Goldman Sachs Trading Corporation. This fund was operated under the same premise as the modern-day closed-end mutual fund. Stock was sold in the Trading Corporation just like any company. The Trading Corporation used the proceeds to buy securities of other companies, with the market price of the fund's shares theoretically determined by the value of the securities held.

The initial capital of the fund consisted of $100 million. Ten million dollars came from the Goldman partners; the rest came from the proceeds of stock sold to the public. For its 10 percent stake, Goldman Sachs completely controlled the fund. The stock offering of the Trading Corporation brought $104 per share, a $4 premium to the fund's initial asset value of $100 per share.

The fund then went out and bought stock of industrial companies. However, as financial writer Benjamin J. Stein described in a February 1991 article in *Barron's*, Goldman Sachs Trading Corporation also bought stock of several commercial banks and insurance companies. (Investment bankers were allowed to have an ownership interest in commercial banks during this period.) Goldman then had the banks and insurance companies use their funds to purchase the securities that

Goldman underwrote for industrial clients.[*][**]

The result was a guaranteed system of securities distribution and demand. With the banks buying securities underwritten by Goldman, and the insurance companies buying securities underwritten by Goldman, and the industrial companies buying securities underwritten by Goldman, and Goldman Sachs Trading Corporation buying securities underwritten by Goldman, there was a ready buyer for every Goldman-underwritten issue.[***]

In this process, the Trading Corporation was making great use of financial leverage. To further take advantage of leverage, the Trading Corporation set up other funds, which were also for the purpose of buying and holding securities. Soon a leveraged fund controlled a leveraged fund that controlled a leveraged fund. In fact, at one point, Goldman Sachs Trading Corporation had control over more than $1.5 *billion* of resources. And remember that the partners had originally put up just $10 million.

The Trading Corporation was a big success—at first. Its share price soon rose to more than $220.

However, in all speculative eras, at some point investors realize that the prices of securities no longer have any relation to their value. Then the music stops. The 1929 stock-market crash helped do that for Goldman's mutual fund. By the spring of 1932, the shares of Goldman Sachs Trading Corporation had lost 99 percent of their maximum value.

Investors were livid. With trust in the partnership greatly diminished, Goldman's securities-distribution network was severely impaired; the firm did not lead a major corporate underwriting until

---

[*] Benjamin J. Stein, "You Can Bank on It: Without Glass-Steagall, History Will Repeat," *Barron's*, February 4, 1991, pp. 16–17.

[**] Commercial banks could readily invest in corporate securities prior to 1933.

[***] This discussion of activities of Goldman Sachs Trading Corporation and Goldman Sachs is for analysis purposes only. It is in no way meant to imply or infer that any of the activities of Goldman Sachs Trading Corporation or Goldman Sachs described herein were illegal.

the mid-1930s. Goldman's partners, including the new head of the firm, Sidney Weinberg, learned a valuable lesson: one must tread very carefully during a leverage craze.

Numerous changes occurred in underwriting in the 1930s. One of the most important involved the role of commercial banks, for such firms weren't exactly angels when it came to this practice.

Prior to 1933, commercial banks were allowed to underwrite corporate securities. However, the banks had often received the leftovers of underwriting, as these firms lacked the distribution networks that houses such as Goldman had been developing for nearly thirty years. Hence, the commercial banks often had to scramble to find buyers for the securities they did sell. The result was a variety of exploits. These included having securities affiliates push risky issues (such as South American bonds) or the stock of the bank itself on customers.

The result of the underwriting practices and the stock-market crash was sweeping legislation. The Glass-Steagall Act of 1933 prohibited commercial banks from the underwriting of corporate securities and the ownership of common stock. Thus, such firms suddenly had to decide whether they wanted to be a commercial bank or an underwriter. Given that the banks had mostly received the low end of the underwriting business, it was no decision at all for them. Every one of the major commercial banks stayed in commercial banking.

Out of that collective decision arose what would become two of the largest investment-banking houses. Personnel of Morgan Bank started the investment-banking firm of Morgan Stanley. The underwriting departments of several commercial banks, including Chase and First National Bank of Boston, came together to create the firm of First Boston.

The exit of the commercial banks left investment-banking firms with the underwriting business to themselves. Hence, the world of underwriting suddenly had greatly reduced competition. With

Goldman and many other houses still suffering from the effects of the 1929 crash, a few of the stronger firms became dominant. Utilizing their connections with corporate managements, a group of investment-banking firms solidified a system for the origination of securities offerings.

The result was a well-defined hierarchy of underwriting. At the top were the dominant houses who led securities offerings. Since this was a small and oligopolistic group, such firms were able to take a large portion of the fees for managing an issue.

These lead firms would distribute a portion of the securities themselves, selling their share to a few large clients. The rest of the issue would then be parceled out to other houses through highly stratified layers in the syndicate. And because each participant depended on the originating firms to give it business—in the form of a share of the syndicate—upward mobility was limited.

Goldman was not one of the dominant underwriters, unfortunately, as the years of hierarchy consolidation coincided with the down period of the firm. During this time, the partnership was led by Sidney Weinberg.

Weinberg brought Goldman out of its post-mutual-fund malaise by following a client-driven practice. He courted the captains of industry and government. By being the friend of corporate leaders, he had a seat on more than 20 boards of directors. Weinberg repaired the image of Goldman in the eyes of clients by convincing them they could trust the firm.

By the 1960s, Goldman had gained back respect. The firm was now a significant underwriter, thanks in part to an advantage provided by its historic strength in commercial paper.

Commercial paper is short-term financing (a company's short-term IOU, which is purchased by an investor). It therefore requires frequent contact between the company and the dealer. In the course of their regular contact with client companies, Goldman people not only assisted with short-term financing needs; they also learned of long-term financing plans. This communication advantage allowed

22 THE DILEMMA

Goldman to be first in line when it came time for an underwriting job. It also helped in securing other services that investment bankers were now beginning to emphasize, such as advising on mergers and acquisitions ("M&A").

The merger activity of the 1960s spawned another attractive business. Gustave (Gus) Levy, Goldman's legend among traders, put the firm into the fast-developing practice of takeover-stock arbitrage.

The definition of arbitrage, whether it be in takeover stocks, currency, or used cars, is simply the use of an information advantage for profit. In other words, a trader sees X selling at $10, but knows that someone will pay $12 for X. The trader buys at $10 and sells at $12. He uses his information (that the seller doesn't know there is a buyer at $12 and the buyer doesn't know there is a seller at $10) to make a quick profit.

In takeover-stock arbitrage, the arbitrageur ("arb") will normally start buying shares either (a) when he suspects an offer for a company is imminent or (b) just after a deal is announced. The stock of the target company will rise on the announcement of a deal, but usually not to the price offered by the acquirer. That's because there is always uncertainty whether the deal will be completed. The arb is generally betting that the transaction will succeed or that an even higher price will be offered by another bidder.

By the late 1960s, Goldman was once again a leading firm on Wall Street. However, Sidney Weinberg passed away in 1969. Shortly thereafter, the firm's image suffered a serious blow.

If you ever want to make a Goldman old-timer cringe, just mention one name: *Penn Central.*

In the late 1960s, Penn Central was an acquisition-minded railroad/conglomerate. Unfortunately, this once high-flying company was having financial difficulties, which were exacerbated by the unfavorable economic climate of 1970.

Goldman Sachs was Penn Central's commercial-paper dealer. Commercial paper, it should be noted, is totally unsecured debt. The holder is in effect saying to the issuing company, "I'll loan you money strictly on your word that you'll pay me back in a few months, no other questions asked or strings attached." A relatively favorable financial outlook is required to issue such debt.

Regardless of its own immediate outlook, Penn Central would need to keep issuing commercial paper to fund its operations. Goldman kept selling Penn Central commercial paper.

Penn Central's finances continued to deteriorate. In June of 1970, Penn Central Transportation Company became the largest corporate bankruptcy to that date. Goldman's customers were left holding commercial paper they had paid $82 million for and now was virtually worthless.

Numerous lawsuits were filed against Goldman. In testimony by Gus Levy (who had taken over the leadership of Goldman), it was revealed that the firm had possessed significant nonpublic information about Penn Central's financial condition that had not been disclosed to commercial-paper customers. After an investigation, the SEC stated that Goldman had learned of critical problems regarding Penn Central that had not been communicated to commercial-paper customers or thoroughly investigated. Over the next several years, Goldman would be forced to resolve dozens of claims against it regarding Penn Central commercial paper.

It would take a while for the Penn Central episode to blow over. When Gus Levy died suddenly in 1976, Goldman was a firm with capital of less than $100 million. But the partners of Goldman Sachs had something significant in their favor: the lessons of Sidney Weinberg.

2. A Tree Grows on Broad Street

In the 1970s, environmental factors caused a break-up of the investment-banking hierarchy. The changes that resulted played right into Goldman's strengths.

The historic change for the securities industry came on May 1, 1975. "May Day" marked the end of fixed commissions on stock transactions.

Prior to May Day, brokerage fees were charged according to a fixed schedule. Since these rates were somewhat generous (for the broker), the brokerage business was quite prosperous, as there was no way for outsiders to break in based on price competition.

After May Day, however, there was real competition. The effect was immediate price slashing. By 1978, stock commissions had been cut to the bone. Financial institutions were paying as little as 5 cents per share on large trades, or only about one-quarter of the old rates.

With the end of fixed commissions, the securities firms that depended on brokerage business were without their built-in moneymaker. Many firms were now forced to hustle for new business in order to survive. And when survival is in question, former practices are discarded. There was an end to the attitude that investment bankers didn't pursue one another's customers. The struggling firms didn't care about status in the underwriting syndicates—the issue now was basic existence. The result was greatly increased competition, which soon forced all investment-banking firms to search for new revenue sources.

The scramble for business in the wake of May Day led to a new breed on Wall Street. In an effort to be more aggressive, the major firms started recruiting a different type of employee. These new investment bankers were hungry, ambitious people. Because their position didn't depend on social connections, they weren't afraid to be aggressive in pursuing business.

The new style of investment banker encountered a new type of corporate financial manager. Gone was the executive who relied extensively on the advice of his investment banker. In his place appeared people with MBAs who had considerable knowledge of financial markets. The combination of Wall Street competitiveness and the increased savvy of corporate financial managements resulted in the breakdown of the hierarchy of underwriting. A watershed event occurred in 1979.

While planning a debt offering, IBM made a surprising request. The firm asked its traditional lead underwriter, Morgan Stanley, to use another firm as co-manager of the issue, in this case Salomon Brothers. It was felt that Salomon Brothers' bond network would help in the efficient distribution of the issue.

The idea that IBM would try to dictate how an offering should be managed was a blow to the status of a lead underwriter like Morgan Stanley, which refused to share the issue with Salomon. So IBM's management came up with another idea: they replaced Morgan Stanley with Merrill Lynch.

From then on, it was every firm for itself in underwriting. Investment bankers began to aggressively compete for underwriting clients. Large corporations obtained a reduction in underwriting fees, and began to employ investment bankers on a transaction-by-transaction basis.

The search for new revenue sources led investment bankers to pursue mergers-and-acquisitions (M&A) work. In 1974, a landmark deal initiated a new era in M&A.

Inco, a large metals firm, made an uninvited tender offer for the shares of ESB (Electric Storage Battery). When the ensuing battle—which featured investment bankers playing key roles—was won by Inco, the hostile bid had been verified as a practical method of M&A.*

The changes revolutionizing investment banking continued into the 1980s. In 1982 the Securities and Exchange Commission adopted Rule 415, which created "shelf registration" of securities. This allowed a company to file a registration statement regarding future financings, then offer the securities at the company's discretion.

The result of shelf registration was a shift in the skills required of underwriters. No longer did clients need to be carefully nursed through the planning and registration of an issue. Instead, value from underwriters now came from the ability to quickly sell the pre-registered securities when the opportune moment arrived.

Meanwhile, M&A hit a new high in 1982 with the epic Bendix Corporation versus Martin Marietta Corporation clash. The celebrated affair started when Bendix made an unwelcome offer for Martin Marietta. Martin Marietta countered with the "Pac-Man" defense (named for a popular video game of the day), launching an offer for Bendix. Soon United Technologies and Allied Corporation joined the fray. Eventually Allied acquired the initial aggressor Bendix, and Martin Marietta escaped.

---

* It is generally considered that a "hostile" offer to purchase a company is one made directly to the shareholders, rather than through the board of directors. (It should be mentioned that at the time of the Inco/ESB affair, the term *hostile offer* was not fully accepted in the lexicon of M&A. While ESB characterized Inco's offer as hostile, Inco denied this.)

The Bendix/Martin Marietta conflict provided an arena for the many investment bankers involved. Tense strategy battles were played out with spy-like intrigue. Martin Marietta and Bendix bought large amounts of each other's shares, which made takeover-stock arbitragers important in the contest. Best of all, there were enormous (for the time) advisory fees, including a reported $7 million for First Boston.

The very idea that a conservative firm such as Bendix would use an aggressive M&A approach brought such actions to the forefront. What's more, there was great business in defending against uninvited suitors. Without question, M&A had gained status as a full-fledged discipline of investment banking.

The result of the events of 1974 through 1982 was the upheaval of the investment-banking community. There were numerous bankruptcies and forced mergers among securities firms; the list of leading investment bankers at the end of this period was significantly changed from the tally at the beginning. One firm was ready—and took advantage of the situation to move to the top of the list.

Goldman gained new clients in the 1970s and climbed into the top tier in underwriting. What's more, shelf registration paid off nicely for the firm.

As mentioned, in shelf registration, the underwriting talent that counted was the ability to distribute securities quickly. That no longer meant working through an intricate syndication. Efficiency in distribution now meant having the institutional contacts to which an issue could be sold posthaste, sometimes in just a few hours. A trading network with institutional-investor clients (i.e., pension funds, mutual funds, insurance companies) became the key. This trend played right into Goldman's strength: if there was one thing the firm possessed, it was institutional customers.

Goldman took advantage of other opportunities emerging out of the revolution in investment banking. There was great potential in M&A advice, and the firm would become a major player. But such status wouldn't come from advising CEOs (chief executive officers) to attempt hostile offers. The firm didn't have to do that, for it already had an advantage in M&A.

With the Penn Central fiasco fading from memory and Goldman building renewed trust in the eyes of its clients, the firm was well-positioned in M&A. CEOs were suspicious of M&A advisors after Bendix/Martin Marietta. When considering an acquisition or merger, a CEO wanted to be certain that an advisor wouldn't turn around and lead an assault on his company.

There had always been the impression that Goldman wouldn't become involved in a deal if it compromised a client relationship. In the early 1980s, this position began to be defined in regard to M&A: Goldman leaders made statements that the firm *would not assist a client in actions that could lead to a hostile deal.*

It wasn't that this policy was put forth for some self-righteous reason. It was simply that hostile actions were bad for long-term business. As Goldman's leaders would publicly state, unfriendly offers (at the time) usually lost (witness Bendix). And when a client loses out on the deal, there aren't a whole lot of fees or feelings of adoration generated for the investment banker. Yet regardless of the reason for the policy, the "no hostile" pledge helped create an important aura of trust.

Goldman was the perfect firm for a CEO to use for M&A guidance. There was no firm more trusted to tell a board of directors that a deal was in the best interest of their company. And if a deal became a clash of egos, no firm was better at handling the situation than the experts from Goldman, whose own partnership was based on sublimating egos to work as a team.

Goldman's renewed image of trust—combined with the growing suspicion of other investment bankers—put the firm in an incredibly enviable position in 1982. Amazingly, the firm represented *both sides* in two large mergers! When Connecticut General Insurance combined with INA Corporation to form Cigna Corporation in a $4 billion deal, Goldman people sat on both sides of the table. The firm was in the same position when Morton-Norwich merged with Thiokol Corporation to create Morton Thiokol.*

Goldman was getting work on many of the large deals. The firm advised Occidental Petroleum on its $4 billion purchase of Cities Service. It advised Heublein when that firm was bought for $1.6 billion by R.J. Reynolds. But the landmark assignment was the mammoth $6 billion merger of U.S. Steel and Marathon Oil. Now it was storied old U.S. Steel—created by J.P. Morgan himself—that had employed Goldman for advice in one of the steelmaker's most important strategic actions.

At the close of 1983, Goldman Sachs was at the top of its game. The firm continued to be a leader in commercial paper. It was in the top three in underwriting volume of corporate securities. It ranked at or near the top in all measures of M&A advisory services. The firm had more than a thousand clients, including such blue-chip firms as General Electric, Ford, Procter & Gamble, and Sears.

Most important, Goldman was winning in the best way for the long run, a way that Gus Levy had once described as being "long-term greedy." The firm was fashioning markets and creating competitive advantages, thereby allowing it to fully capitalize on its chosen ventures. The result was amazing financial performance.

When Gus Levy passed away in 1976, the partnership is estimated to have been earning approximately $70 million of annual pre-tax profit, and had capital of about $90 million. In 1983, Goldman was estimated to have earned $400 million, and partners' capital stood at $502 million at year-end.**

---

* In the Connecticut General/INA Corporation merger, Connecticut General was also advised by Lazard Freres and INA was also advised by Lehman Brothers. In the Morton-Norwich/Thiokol Corporation merger, Morton-Norwich was also advised by Salomon Brothers and Thiokol was also advised by Lazard Freres. (It is not illegal or unethical for an M&A advisor to represent both sides in a merger.)

** Partners' capital is the equity of a partnership. The partners own interests in the equity, but such capital usually remains in the firm until a partner leaves and requests his share. Being a private partnership, Goldman does not publicly disclose its earnings. However, the firm's profits during this period could be reasonably estimated based on capital levels and other measures Goldman is required to report. Also, partnership profits are not taxed in the manner of corporate income, but are taxed at the individual partner level.

Most amazing was the relative profitability of Goldman. For Wall Street firms, a 25 percent pre-tax return on equity is good. Thirty-five percent is outstanding. Fifty percent is phenomenal. However, if one divides the $400 million profit that Goldman was estimated to have made in 1983 by the average level of partners' capital during the year (of $432 million), the result is a pre-tax return on equity in excess of 90 percent. And the firm's income was shared by just 73 general partners.

The Goldman partnership had everything going its way. From a new headquarters building at 85 Broad Street, the firm's people could look down on the financial world they held reign over. Unfortunately, in the next year and a half, things would turn sour.

3. The Milken Arriveth

It wasn't a complete surprise. The storm clouds warning of the fury of Michael Milken's junk bonds—and the hostile-takeover bids and leveraged buyouts they would spawn—had been forming for the past three years.*

The junk-debt market was developed slowly during the late 1970s and early 1980s. In 1983, however, Milken's baby arrived. A stir was created when Drexel, which was never more than a minor competitor in the past, suddenly challenged the top five of underwriting on the strength of more than $4 billion of public junk-debt volume.**

Meanwhile, there were several players who were using hostile tactics to obtain "greenmail" from scared companies. One of the most notable was Carl Icahn, who frightened several firms in the early 1980s and amassed profits of more than $40 million in the process.***

---

* "Junk" bonds are debt securities rated Ba1 or lower by Moody's or BB+ or lower by Standard & Poor's rating services, in contrast to higher-rated "investment grade" debt.

** The leaders in underwriting were Morgan Stanley, Salomon Brothers, Merrill Lynch, Goldman Sachs, and First Boston.

*** The 1980s term *greenmail* came to refer to a range of concepts. In the narrowest definition, greenmail occurred when a company purchased the stockholdings of an unwanted suitor at a price above market in return for the abandonment of the suitor's actions. However, in a broader sense, greenmail involved a company's purchase of any securities from any party at any price (under the threat of antagonistic action by the party) in a deal not available to other holders of the same class of securities.

32 THE DILEMMA

It didn't take a genius to see that Milken and the "takeover artists" would eventually come together. In late 1983, it happened. In a huge warning shot of things to come, an investor group led by Mesa Petroleum chairman T. Boone Pickens Jr., ostensibly backed by Drexel-arranged financing, began a series of hostile rumblings against Gulf Oil. Incredibly, Drexel was able to put together enough financing commitments that Pickens' challenge was taken seriously. Gulf Oil was ultimately acquired by white knight Chevron in a $13.2 billion deal, the largest M&A transaction to that point.* And while it was somewhat doubtful that Drexel could have financed a takeover, the potential power of junk debt had been demonstrated. What's more, the Mesa group had a $214 million profit on its Gulf holdings.

There was another significant but less-remembered aspect of the battle for Gulf, which was the attempt of Kohlberg Kravis Roberts ("KKR") to acquire the oil firm in a leveraged buyout ("LBO"). Entering the bidding at the eleventh hour, KKR made a competitive proposal. Most amazing, the LBO firm was able to line up $6 billion in commercial-bank financing.**

The KKR bid for Gulf was important for another reason. The LBO firm's proposal included a large amount of an unusual type of financing, which would become popular in 1980s bids.

In KKR's bid, which had a face value of more than $80 per share, only $48.75 per share was in cash. The rest of the offer consisted of debt and preferred-stock securities to be given directly to Gulf shareholders (and repaid from future cash flows of Gulf).

In M&A terminology, such instruments are known as "cram down" securities. That's because the securities are "forced down the throat" of the shareholder as part of the purchase price. In the past, cram-down financing had been frowned upon. After all, by making such an offer, a bidder is really saying to shareholders, "I'll buy your com-

---

* A "white knight" is a company that is invited to acquire (and thus rescue) a firm that is the target of an unwanted takeover attempt by a third company.

** The term *LBO firm* will be used in reference to entities that organize, arrange financing for, and take controlling equity positions in leveraged buyouts (such as Kohlberg Kravis Roberts), as opposed to the firm actually acquired in an LBO.

pany, provided you lend me the money." Yet even though KKR lost out to Chevron's all-cash bid, the key point was that the LBO firm's offer was considered quite legitimate.

Other events were bringing leveraged buyouts into the news. The deal that grabbed everyone's attention was William Simon's success with Gibson Greetings. An investment firm led by Simon acquired the greeting-card company in an LBO in 1982 for $80 million. When a public stock offering was done of Gibson Greetings eighteen months later for $290 million, Simon's personal equity stake, which cost $330,000, was worth $66 million. In other words, *a 200-to-1 return.* And while Gibson Greetings was a relatively small deal, managements of large firms became interested in this financial tactic when John Kluge, chairman of Metromedia, did a $1.1 billion LBO of that company in early 1984.

So what exactly is a leveraged buyout, that financial strategy that epitomized the 1980s?

LBOs, originally known as "bootstrap financings," had been done for years in small deals. Basically, a leveraged buyout is the purchase of a company by an investor group (which usually includes the management of the firm being acquired) using a large amount of debt as funding.

The financing structure varies for each deal, but generally (at least back in the early 1980s) the acquirers put up about 10 percent of the purchase price in cash as equity in the deal. The rest of the purchase price (i.e., 90 percent or more) is borrowed. The buyout group then pays down the debt over time by (a) selling off operations that can bring prices greater than the value of the cash flows being generated by those operations and (b) extracting as much cash flow as possible out of the rest of the company.*

---

*The important point to remember about the LBO capital structure is that the higher the percentage of debt (and thus the lower the percentage of equity), the greater the leverage and the higher the return on the equity. A 10 percent return on equity in an unleveraged (unlevered) firm becomes a 100 percent return on equity in a firm that has a 9:1 ratio of debt to equity. This is precisely the concept of financial "leverage," as debt is used as a lever to increase the return of the equity.

The ability to generate cash to pay off debt is the key to an LBO. Such a financial structure is therefore best suited to companies that have strong, stable cash flow and minimal capital-expenditure needs. It is also good if there is excess cash on the balance sheet at the time of the buyout, as such money can be used to offset acquisition debt—and thus help fund the deal. All the better if there are any surplus assets, such as unused real estate, that can be quickly sold to reduce debt.

Often after only a couple years of selling operations and squeezing out cash, much of the buyout debt will have been paid off. If values in the M&A market have been going up in the interim (as was the case throughout the mid-1980s), what remains of the company can be sold or "taken public" in an equity offering for a good price. Since the buyout group gets to pocket all of the proceeds in excess of any remaining debt, their initial sliver of equity can be worth many times the original investment (witness Gibson Greetings).

There is an important rule of thumb on LBO pricing. This rule states that it is usually safe to pay a purchase price of a certain multiple, depending on prevailing interest rates, of the expected annual cash flow of the acquired firm. In the 1980s, the rule of thumb was about five- to six-times cash flow. The point is that a price significantly greater than the prudent multiple means that, in order to service the excessive acquisition debt, the buyer has to do one or both of two things: (a) quickly sell off a large amount of operations at high prices or (b) greatly improve cash flow.[*]

The initial LBOs were done at rational prices, mainly because these deals tended to be quite private affairs. The early buyouts also were financed mostly with loans secured by the value of the assets acquired.

However, as deals became larger and more competitive, prices went higher and equity layers got slimmer. LBOs soon required a

---

[*] Cash flow in this case means "operating" cash flow, the amount of cash generated each year from the normal operations of a business. This is defined as earnings before interest and taxes ("EBIT") plus depreciation (depreciation being added back because it is a non-cash expense). Thus this measure is also referred to as "EBITD."

layer of debt between the secured loans and the equity. This middle layer became known as the "mezzanine" tier of financing, as it was above the "bottom floor" of the capital structure (the equity) and below the "top story" (the senior debt).

Being unsecured and subordinated, mezzanine debt was the trickiest of all the financing. Senior loans and equity were easy to obtain. Venturesome banks came running to make asset-based LBO loans in the early 1980s: such debt provided interest rates two to three percentage points above the prime rate and juicy fees of as much as one percent of the loan. And given the promise of huge returns such as Gibson Greetings, there was always plenty of money for equity. But the mezzanine lender was stuck with just plain risky debt. As a result, he demanded a high interest rate and, almost always, a portion of the equity.

In the early years, institutional investors such as insurance companies often funded the mezzanine layer. Such an arrangement was fine for carefully negotiated private deals; however, by 1984, LBOs were moving into the public arena. To acquire a publicly traded company, an LBO organizer needed to get the deal done quickly, before other bidders jumped in.

Hence, the key to such deals was the ability to swiftly raise large amounts of subordinated debt to fill in the mezzanine layer. And there was a firm with the perfect tool for this task—which was becoming acquainted with LBO firms. Its name was Drexel Burnham.

Prior to this time, corporate takeovers were almost always done by large companies that possessed huge resources. Smaller entities usually couldn't accomplish such deals, as they couldn't arrange the necessary financing.

However, with the arrival of junk-bond financing, there was now greatly increased deal potential. Junk bonds could be used to fund the mezzanine layer in LBOs. These securities could also be used to back hostile-takeover efforts. The viability of junk debt in such actions drew in more commercial-bank funding. The result was that it was now possible for smaller entities to initiate large takeover/LBO actions, and by 1984 there appeared a group of financial innovators attempting to exploit the new leverage possibilities.

By 1985, the Drexel machine was really rolling. Besides the Gulf Oil affair, the power of junk bonds had been used by Saul Steinberg to make Walt Disney Productions tremble and by tiny Leucadia National to frighten Avco Corporation. But now, in addition to scaring companies into buying back stock or seeking a white knight, Milken's tool was being used to actually complete huge leveraged acquisitions. Ronald Perelman's Pantry Pride took over Revlon for $1.8 billion, Coastal Corporation acquired American National Resources for $2.5 billion, and Carl Icahn gained control of TWA, all made possible through Drexel-raised financing. Milken's system also helped fund large LBOs, including the $1.0 billion buyout of Uniroyal by Clayton & Dubilier and the $2.4 billion purchase of Storer Communications by KKR. Even relatively unknown players suddenly had the power to complete large deals, as William Farley acquired Northwest Industries for $1.2 billion and Nelson Peltz and Peter May's Triangle Industries purchased National Can.

The key to this world of takeovers and LBOs was quick financing, and in 1985, Drexel Burnham was the only firm that had it. Drexel was the linchpin in leveraged transactions. The firm was able to charge fees of three percent to four percent of the value of a junk-bond issue (versus the less than one percent charged on investment-grade debt), and large fees for "M&A advice" as well. Though the takeover and LBO players were receiving most of the publicity, they were but an agent for the man who controlled the action. The leverage game was nothing without Michael Milken.

How did Milken gain such power? He did it by creating a controlled system of securities distribution and demand.

It began by gaining access to a large pool of funds; specifically, the money of mutual funds (e.g., First Investors Fund for Income), savings-and-loans (e.g., Columbia Savings and Loan), and insurance companies (e.g., First Executive Corporation). Milken helped raise financing for such entities; he also convinced their managements to invest in junk-rated securities. Many of the junk-bond issues these entities invested in were used to finance bids by takeover players. To complete the loop, the profits and liquid resources of many of the takeover players were then invested in the securities of the other participants in the system. Because all of the major participants greatly desired junk-debt financing and/or investment opportunities, they dutifully played the game.

But think about this. Milken's system was nothing new. It was really just the standard method for taking advantage of a leverage craze, remarkably like the one used in the Goldman Sachs Trading Corporation design of the 1920s. Consider the following similarities.*

In both cases, access was gained to a large pool of funds. In the Goldman design, a mutual fund was created that bought interests in commercial banks and insurance companies.

The Milken system also utilized mutual funds and insurance companies. And while commercial banks weren't permitted to invest in junk bonds, deregulation allowed the next-best purchaser in savings-and-loans.

These entities then provided a guaranteed system of securities demand/distribution. In the Goldman design, the entities bought securities issued by industrial clients. In Milken's system, the entities purchased securities issued by clients doing leveraged deals of industrial firms. The result was that, in both cases, there were plenty of ready buyers providing demand for new issues.

A major reward for both Goldman in the 1920s and Drexel in the 1980s was fees from underwriting and merger work, plus trading profits. But there were also rewards from the equity in the systems. For Goldman it had been the appreciation in the prices of securities held by the mutual funds, enhanced through a chain of leverage.

---

* This comparison is for analysis purposes only regarding the subject of financial leverage. It is in no way meant to imply or infer that Goldman Sachs or Goldman Sachs Trading Corporation was involved in illegal acts such as those of Michael Milken, Drexel Burnham, or others, or that Goldman Sachs was involved in the Drexel/Milken system.

Milken took equity warrants from junk-bond issuers. He kept many of the warrants within the firm, and spread the rest around as a reward for clients. Warrants were perfect in this function. These instruments appeared to have little cost for the issuer, while providing the holder with a claim on the immense wealth potential of leveraged-deal equity.

By early 1985, Drexel was in command. Companies were buying back stock and submitting to defenses to escape the actions of the junk-financed players. Managements of public companies and the persons who worked in corporate headquarters lived in constant fear of a hostile-takeover bid. Vulnerable firms began to continuously monitor the trading in their stock. The *Wall Street Journal* became a thick and frightening volume for corporate executives, as huge leveraged deals and brazen takeover attempts were announced every week.

This situation was less than ideal for Goldman. Although a few hostile actions now and then are good—forcing companies to the investment banker for defense advice and providing nice fees—general hostilities driven by an instrument that only one firm possessed were bad. The repeated victories by the junk-financed players were disheartening. The most that Goldman could get out of such affairs (as in the acquisitions of American National Resources and Northwest Industries) were modest fees for advising the targets on how best to be acquired.

Yet defense of corporate clients would be the chosen course for Goldman, the ideal way to utilize the trust it had earned. All Goldman needed was an effective maneuver to use against junk-financed foes.

The current defenses were things such as stock buybacks, various legal maneuvers, and arranging a white knight. Unfortunately, these tactics were now virtually impotent against Milken's tool. In early 1985 Drexel devised the "highly confident" letter, which assured that a deal could be quickly funded with junk securities. And it could. Thus by the time a company tried a standard defense, its shares might be long gone to a takeover player making an offer backed by highly confident currency. In the early 1980s, hostile offers usually didn't win; that was one of the main reasons Goldman took the role of defender. By 1985, hostile offers could win—and did win—when financed with junk debt.

A clever victory versus a junk-financed foe would go a long way in establishing Goldman as the premier defender in the new takeover world, the firm that all worried managements should come to for advice. Such an opportunity came about in early 1985, when Boone Pickens went after another oil company, this time huge Unocal.

The Unocal affair started in February 1985. It was announced that a Pickens investor group, Mesa Partners (II), had bought stock of the oil giant. Although he had never actually taken over a major company, Pickens possessed a large bankroll from the Gulf Oil affair and smaller victories, plus some credit lines left over from a recent joust with Phillips Petroleum. By the end of March, Mesa Partners had spent $1.1 billion to acquire 13.6 percent of Unocal's shares.

If Pickens wanted to pick a fight with the toughest of opponents, he had succeeded. Unocal's chairman, Fred Hartley, had never been a man in need of assertiveness training.

When Hartley was the young president of the oil firm in 1965, the company had—under the threat of antagonistic action—repurchased a sizeable holding from shipping tycoon Daniel Ludwig. Ludwig reaped a $45 million profit in the bargain.* Thus one could understand that Hartley wasn't exactly enthralled with the tactics of Drexel's takeover clients.

Mesa soon announced a tender offer to acquire Unocal shares for $54 per share. The bid was of the type still prevalent in that pre-poison-pill era, the infamous "two-step" offer.

Pickens' group offered cash for 37 percent of the shares of Unocal. When combined with the 13.6 percent that Mesa Partners already held, this would give it a controlling 50 percent-plus position. That was Step One.

---

* Ludwig's shares were repurchased at the market price.

In Step Two, Mesa would pay $54 per share for the remaining 49 percent of Unocal's stock. However, the payment in Step Two would not be in cash, but instead would be in debt securities. The total value of the deal would be roughly $9 billion.

The point of a two-step offer was simple. The idea was to convince shareholders to tender quickly in order to get their payment in the first step, and thereby receive cash. That was because the shareholders who waited and ended up with debt securities from the second payment risked getting less.

You see, it often wasn't certain what the second payment in a two-step would be worth. For example, the acquirer might be paying too much for the target, and thus might not be able to service the debt securities. There might not be a liquid market in the securities. In the end, the two-step offer was nothing other than the old pressure tactic of "I'll pay a guaranteed cash price to those who act now—while those who wait are taking their chances." Consequently, all shareholders were given incentive to tender fast.

Mesa's offer was bold, but the most amazing part was the financing behind it. A little more than $3 billion would be needed to fund the Step-One share purchases. Yet the money was instantly arranged! In just one week from the date the Mesa offer was announced, Drexel had received commitments from participants in its financing system for *$3 billion*. And Mesa Partners lined up another $900 million in bank credit.

Drexel's financing prowess was astounding. With its Step-One funding in place, Mesa was a serious threat. Unless there were a meaningful response by Unocal, the stockholders—especially the arbitragers—would likely tender their shares. Unocal was against the wall.

Who could Fred Hartley, a man known to not exactly have great affection for investment bankers, possibly use for defense advice? There was a perfect choice: the trusted advisor who avoided any role in promoting hostile deals. Unocal called on Goldman Sachs.

Unocal needed some imaginative thinking to thwart Pickens, for its options were limited. The company might try to find a white knight, as Gulf had done. However, there were few oil firms capable of acquiring Unocal. And Hartley had stated that Unocal wasn't for sale.

Unocal's management could attempt a leveraged buyout, with Goldman raising the money. But this would be a huge leveraged deal. Arranging the mezzanine financing through normal institutional channels could take weeks or even months. Unocal needed a solution in a matter of days. Furthermore, Hartley had publicly criticized LBOs.

Although it seemed Unocal was in serious trouble, the company and its advisors had a response. Soon after Mesa's $54-per-share offer was made, Unocal sprung the plan, an incredibly clever turn of the tables.

Unocal announced an innovative plan to repurchase stock. The deal was simple: If (and only if) Mesa Partners succeeded in acquiring more than 50 percent, Unocal would then offer to buy back the remaining 49 percent of its shares. However, the payment in the Unocal offer would be an astronomical *$72 per share.*

What's more, the buyback payment would not be in cash. Instead, it would be in the form of the oil company's debt—specifically, senior secured notes. In other words, no financing would have to be arranged. Unocal would just repurchase shares with its own "paper" (i.e., securities).

The Unocal plan put Pickens in a bit of a bind. If he went through with Step One of the tender offer, he risked ending up with a company loaded with debt, including more than $4 billion of his own acquisition debt and $6 billion from the Unocal buyback. Yet it would be difficult to do anything substantive, such as selling the assets that secured the buyback debt, in order to extract cash from the oil company.

Furthermore, Pickens' group couldn't simply tender its shares to the buyback and take a $72-per-share payment, as the Unocal offer would occur only if Mesa Partners first acquired more than 50 percent. And since Mesa Partners had already purchased more than 10 percent of Unocal's stock, securities law restricted it from selling its stake right away.*

Unocal and Goldman had turned around the two-step and made it work to the advantage of the target company. But while the Unocal plan was ingenious, one might also observe that the tactic was somewhat of a scorched-earth approach. If Pickens acquired an overleveraged Unocal, it was no good for him, but it was also no good for the oil company.

In reality, however, it was unlikely that Unocal would have to implement its repurchase plan. The strategy was designed to be a clever bluff—a blocking move, a checkmate—which would compel Pickens to drop his tender offer. In fact, that's what made the plan so great: Unocal's strategy could defeat Pickens without the oil company incurring any debt or cost at all!

The market seemed to believe the gambit would work, as Unocal's stock price began to drift down. However, this wasn't pleasing the takeover-stock arbitragers (an important constituency in any takeover battle), who now held much of Unocal's stock. The arbs would prefer that the oil company actually carry out some sort of action.

Unocal soon announced a revised buyback plan. The oil company now offered to repurchase 29 percent of its stock (for $72-per-share in securities) regardless of what Pickens did. But a key feature of this revised plan was that the shares owned by Pickens' group *were not included in the repurchase offer.*

The exclusion of Mesa Partners was based on a logical argument. Unocal held that Pickens might be trying to get the oil company to buy back his group's shares at a premium (which would be detrimental to

---

* At 10 percent equity ownership, an investor reaches the threshold at which he automatically becomes an "insider" (even though he may be completely outside the company, as Pickens' group was here). The investor is then subject to the SEC's "short swing" rule, which restricts insiders from buying and then selling their shares (or vice versa) within a six-month period. Thus in 1980s takeover actions, one would usually see a pursuer stop at a 9.9 percent stake before launching an offer.

the other shareholders). Therefore, if takeover players can get companies to buy back shares to the exclusion of the other stockholders, we (Unocal) *can buy back shares from the other stockholders to the exclusion of takeover players.* It was greenmail in reverse!*

Pickens threatened to tender his group's shares anyway and began a legal challenge. The two sides then started to talk. However, the talks broke down. Then the courts ruled that Unocal *could* exclude Mesa Partners from the buyback offer.

That meant Pickens was beaten. He couldn't tender to Unocal's offer, and it wouldn't be worthwhile for Mesa to complete its own tender offer. Pickens' group immediately came calling to strike a truce.

In a bittersweet conclusion, Unocal agreed to a deal. The oil company would buy back 32 percent of Mesa Partner's shares (and a prorated 38 percent of the other stockholders' shares that were tendered to the buyback offer) for $72 per share. Mesa Partners would sell the rest of its holdings, but only over time so as not to depress Unocal's stock.

With the takeover threat now gone, Unocal's stock price dropped below $35. Mesa Partners, which had acquired its shares at an average cost in the mid-$40s, was sitting with at best a breakeven position on its stake. Pickens and his Texas two-step had been one-upped.

Technically, Unocal had won. Goldman's innovative advice had saved the day, stopping a Drexel-financed offensive in its tracks. The $5.3 billion of debt that Unocal now possessed greatly reduced its attractiveness as a target.

But there weren't celebrations at Unocal. There was less than overwhelming joy with the outcome, as CEO Hartley had previously denounced stock buybacks from takeover players. And adding $4

---

* Pickens had denied that he had ever sought or accepted greenmail, and had stated he would not accept such an offer from Unocal. In the past, he had agreed to have holdings bought back by companies, specifically by Cities Service in 1982, Superior Oil in 1983, and Phillips Petroleum in 1985.

billion of debt (as the repurchase had done) doesn't make it any easier to run a business.

It was now clear that a stock buyback, no matter how cleverly packaged, was still a costly maneuver. Consequently, such tactic didn't appear to be the definitive anti-Drexel action. Unocal and Goldman had prevailed in the battle because Hartley wasn't afraid to innovate; this would not be true of lesser executives. The oil company had succeeded by using risky legal tactics. The next client might not be so lucky. Goldman received a decent fee for its Unocal work, reportedly more than $12 million. But this was nothing like the fees that could be made for organizing and financing a full-blown leveraged deal.

However, a bigger reason the Unocal buyback wasn't an attractive defense was, quite simply, that there were no large rewards for management, no chance for leveraged-deal equity returns. What fun is it to just keep one's job?

Goldman had shown it could be resourceful in a defensive role against the best of opponents. Yet the Unocal affair also provided a clear glimpse of the financing strength of Drexel. In this case, the client had won without Goldman having to raise funding to compete with Milken's system; the Unocal buyback was paid for with the oil company's own notes, a type of cram-down security. But could such method defeat a junk-financed player who was bound and determined to take over his target?

The Unocal affair was a plus to Goldman's image as a defender, but it would be preferable to have a tactic that let everyone win. Perhaps there was a more proactive approach.

4. Take My Paper, Please!

Since managements of large companies were now scared of takeover players, it was becoming easier to convince executives to attempt a leveraged buyout. And such tactic might be the perfect defense tool. An LBO could presumably be used to give shareholders a big payday that would defeat a takeover player. Even better, the tactic could be done "preemptively," being enacted prior to any takeover threat. But before such a strategy could be put into action, two hurdles had to be cleared: CEOs needed to be convinced to take the daring plunge, and the LBO organizer had to have the ability to swiftly raise large amounts of debt.

While executives of large companies were desperately worried about the hostile actions going on around them, most were hesitant to risk the upheaval and massive debt of an LBO unless directly threatened. What such executives needed was an example of the enormous wealth potential available to a colleague who was not afraid to take on leverage proactively. The experience of John Kluge and the Metromedia LBO provided just such an illustration.

46 THE DILEMMA

Kluge, who served as an intelligence officer in World War II, started a radio station after the war and eventually became the leader of a company that grew into the communications-giant Metromedia.

In 1984, an investor group that Kluge had formed bought Metromedia in a $1.1 billion LBO. The deal was financed primarily by bank debt, with Prudential Insurance providing a type of mezzanine funding and receiving a piece of the equity. Being the force behind the deal, Kluge himself managed to procure three-quarters of the equity.*

Kluge's plan for the deal soon became clear. About a year after the buyout, Metromedia began selling assets and operations. And with the M&A market heating up, the company obtained fabulous prices for its properties.

Metromedia continued selling assets and paying off debt. Two and a half years after the LBO, there were almost no operating assets remaining. What was left? A cash hoard estimated at almost $2 *billion*. John Kluge had become one of the five-richest men in America.

The Metromedia case seemed to demonstrate a couple of things. Number one, it showed that an LBO of more than $1 billion could be financed by banks and institutional investors before any takeover players moved in. Number two, it showed how underpriced some companies were compared to their value on a leveraged basis or the value of their separate pieces. In buying Metromedia, Kluge's group paid almost double the recent market price of the company's stock. Then it turned out that Metromedia's assets were worth $2 billion more than what Kluge's group had paid. The message to CEOs? Many of you have a drastically undervalued company, which—via the tactic of an LBO—can provide huge personal wealth.

In addition to Kluge's success, other events were spurring on leverage fever. Three large New York banks—Manufacturers Hanover, Citicorp, and Bankers Trust—started to aggressively pursue leveraged-deal loans. These banks were ready sources of senior debt

---

* Kluge owned approximately 25 percent of Metromedia before the LBO.

for LBOs and takeover bids, and quickly became the leaders in bank lending for leveraged deals.*

LBOs could put a client-friendly investment banker at the forefront of the leverage game and bring all the benefits thereof. In addition to being a proactive defense tool for clients, LBOs would allow the investment banker to reap the large fees from mezzanine financing. Another benefit would be M&A fees from the post-buyout divestitures. And in a few years there might be underwriting work if the buyout group decided to do a public offering of the company.

Goldman hit the big time in LBOs in 1985 with R.H. Macy & Company department stores. "Macy's" was prime for a leveraged deal. After having traded near $60 in late 1983, the retailer's stock was languishing in the mid-$40s in the spring of 1985. At such price, the company was valued at only about four-times its cash flow.**

Macy's also possessed "hidden assets," in the form of valuable shopping-center interests. Most important, the company had an ambitious CEO in Edward Finkelstein.

After two months of discussions with Goldman, Finkelstein raised the idea of an LBO at a board-of-directors meeting in June 1985. Finkelstein and several other senior Macy's executives soon joined together to take steps toward proposing a buyout at $68 per share. Following several months of back and forth between the Macy's board and the management group, a plan was approved in January 1986. The $68-per-share deal came to a total price of $3.5 billion.

Goldman and the management group proceeded to go about securing the LBO financing. All went smoothly at first. Citibank and Manufac-

---

* Reference will be made throughout this book to activities of both Citicorp and Citibank, the latter being a subsidiary of the former.

** The cash-flow multiple at which a firm is valued is calculated as follows. Take the total market value of the company's "capitalization" (consisting of the market value of equity [i.e., stock price times shares outstanding] plus the net amount of debt [i.e., debt minus excess cash on hand]) and divide that figure by EBITD.

turers Hanover had provided commitment letters for much of the bank funding. General Electric Credit Corporation had committed to purchase a portion of the mezzanine debt, and would acquire preferred shares convertible into common equity. All that was needed was to wrap up the senior financing and find the rest of the mezzanine money. Armed with a set of growth forecasts for Macy's, Goldman attacked the hungry world of leveraged-deal funding sources.

It was here where it became evident what a financier was up against in the leverage game. For while Drexel could raise billions of dollars for a leveraged deal with seemingly effortless ease, the task wasn't as simple as it looked.

As was mentioned earlier, Goldman had the institutional contacts to move securities quickly. However, that was in traditional securities distribution. Convincing institutions to buy debt from a leveraged deal was a different matter. And while it was true that Milken had convinced a number of institutions of the merits of such debt, that was when it was distributed through Drexel. Investors didn't necessarily want such paper when it was sold through other investment bankers.

A scramble ensued to place the Macy's funding. After four months (a period that would soon be considered an eternity in leveraged-deal time), the financing was substantially complete. The buyout was approved at a shareholder meeting in June 1986.

In the end, however, the Macy's financing was worth the trouble. That's because the deal generated more than $30 million of fees for Goldman.

Even with all the aggravation, this really was easy money. Sure, the financing had been tough. But with a little practice, why, Goldman could make a killing in this game. After all, the firm had just completed the second-largest LBO (behind the Beatrice deal, which was finished while Macy's was in process) of all time.

But while Goldman had succeeded in the Macy's deal, by 1986 the world of leveraged buyouts had changed. One could no longer play the LBO game by patiently placing the debt over a period of weeks or months. The institutional well of financing just wasn't fast enough versus Milken's network of instant funding. Another deal that Goldman was advising on at this time, the National Gypsum LBO, would be quite a bit more educational in this regard.

National Gypsum processes gypsum (the white, chalky stuff that flakes out of your dented garage walls when you're not careful backing out the car) and makes wallboard out of it. In the early 1980s, the fortunes of this company soared by virtue of a construction boom. Housing starts increased from 1.1 million units in 1982 to a 1.7 million-unit level from 1983 through 1985. National Gypsum's annual sales nearly doubled between 1983 and 1985, and its income more than tripled during that period.

Beginning in 1984, certain officers and directors of National Gypsum had discussions with Goldman representatives regarding the feasibility of a leveraged buyout. In November of 1985, a group of senior executives were ready. An LBO proposal was submitted to the board of directors. The management group's offer was $40.50-per-share in cash, plus $17-per-share in "subordinated redeemable discount debentures."

What exactly were the discount debentures that were being offered? One first recognizes them as cram-down securities. Instead of trying to sell this portion of the mezzanine debt in the market, it would simply be given to the shareholders.

There were other significant features of the debentures. The securities were a type of debt known as "split coupon." This meant they would pay no interest for a certain period, five years in this case. The debentures would then pay interest at 15 percent for fifteen years thereafter.

Since the debentures paid no interest for five years, their value obviously was something less than the $17 face amount (i.e., the discount aspect). Based on the financial risk in the deal and the present value of the cash flows to the debtholders, analysts estimated the value of a debenture at about $9.50 (per share). This gave the management group's offer a value of about $50 per share. Since

National Gypsum was on the way to making operating cash flow of $11 per share for 1985 (and had negligible debt, net of its cash balances), the $50-per-share bid was priced at a reasonable 4.5 multiple.

Cram-down securities could be perfect for mezzanine financing in leveraged deals—for such securities are the ultimate in instant financing. In addition, cram-down securities could be useful in a bidding war. If a leveraged-deal bidder needed to raise its price, it could simply add more cram-down debt. And by using deferred-interest securities, the acquirer wouldn't incur any extra cost (in terms of cash interest payments) for several years. It was as if one could print one's own acquisition currency! Now all that had to be determined was whether a board of directors would go for this idea.

A special committee of National Gypsum directors appointed to review the LBO proposal had some concerns about the offer, specifically with the value and marketability of the discount debentures. Thus some minor changes were made in the terms of the debentures.

The National Gypsum board approved a revised proposal on January 7, 1986. A shareholder meeting to vote on the deal was scheduled for April 10. February passed, March passed, and it appeared everything was rounding into shape as the shareholder meeting approached.

Then it happened; a nightmare came true. Two days before the scheduled shareholder vote on the LBO plan, Sanford Sigoloff, CEO of Wickes Companies (a Drexel client), telephoned the National Gypsum chief executive to inform him that Wickes planned to make an all-cash tender offer for the gypsum company's shares for $54 per share. Wickes had already bought a stake in National Gypsum, the maximum it could purchase prior to antitrust clearance, for an average of $49.375 per share.

Wickes appeared to be a serious threat. The firm had recently made a billion-dollar acquisition; thus it seemed to be a legitimate acquirer and not a greenmailer. Wickes had filed a registration for a large debt offering, and now stated that Drexel was "highly confident" it could raise all the financing needed by Wickes for the National Gypsum purchase. National Gypsum immediately delayed the shareholder vote until April 25.

What a letdown for Goldman and the management group. After all the work to arrange the LBO, here was a Drexel-backed player coming in and stealing the show.

The management group countered by increasing the value of the LBO plan. The new offer would pay $46-per-share in cash, plus a $28 (face amount) discount debenture. The management group presented this proposal as financially superior to the Wickes offer. Analysts valued the package at a per-share price in the low $60s.

Sanford Sigoloff now held the fate of the National Gypsum affair in his hands. Wickes eventually made a proposal of $64 per share.

The management group's response was to print up some more acquisition currency by increasing the face value of the discount debentures. This latest offer was ostensibly worth at least $65 per share. National Gypsum's stock price rose above $65.

With an easy profit in hand, Wickes dropped out of the bidding. The firm sold for an average of $68.375 per share the stock it had bought for $49.375—which was quite a nice spread for three weeks' work. The National Gypsum management group thus "won" with its cash-and-debt deal.

But there was some question as to what the LBO group had really won. While the original bid was a reasonable 4.5 multiple of cash flow, the final deal was stretched to six-times cash flow on a cyclical business.

There are key ratios that reveal the risk inherent in an LBO plan. One of the rules of thumb says that in the fifth year of the financial projections for the deal (and no later than the seventh year), debt as a percentage of total capitalization (i.e., total debt plus equity) should be down to 50 percent. A higher percentage indicates that the company may not have the cash-generating potential to safely handle the buyout debt.

Yet the financial projections for the National Gypsum deal showed debt as a percentage of total capitalization still being 90 percent at the end of the seventh year. And for that year, earnings before interest and taxes were projected to only modestly exceed net interest expense. In so many words, this LBO had been pulled a bit thin.

Although Goldman's side had prevailed in the National Gypsum deal, it was becoming difficult for an investment banker to complete prudent LBOs without the ability to quickly place large amounts of leveraged-deal debt in the market. There were now enough Drexel-backed players around that it was likely one would show up to challenge any LBO bid.

Thus, preemptive LBOs might not be the best way for Goldman to compete in the leverage game. The firm didn't have an advantage in this tactic (other than contact with corporate managements) and possessed a mezzanine-financing disadvantage versus Drexel. What would be desirable would be a new and creative tactic in which the firm had an edge.

In 1986, Drexel ruled. Its financing machine hit high gear, with Milken achieving the legendary compensation figure of $550 million for that year.

Drexel was now a real problem. Its clients were acquiring other investment bankers' clients and hindering the rest of Wall Street's own leveraged-deal efforts. Worse yet, the effects of the leverage/takeover boom were spilling into other businesses.

Equity underwriting, a Goldman strength area, was stagnating, as debt had become the financing medium of choice. American companies were leveraging up en masse. Total debt of non-financial corporations increased almost 50 percent between 1983 and 1986.

Goldman's own bond operations were struggling. The firm had been losing customers to aggressive competitors who were undercutting on fees. Goldman's bond-trading unit was headed by what would be the second of three different partners in a span of just nineteen months (in a firm known for stability).

Commercial banks, an important ally of all investment bankers, were becoming a threat. Having seen the immense fees from leveraged-deal financing, several large banks were getting ready to promote M&A services backed by their own instant source of funds. Commercial banks also wanted a piece of other investment-banking businesses. They were trying to get into the underwriting of corporate securities by clamoring for relaxation of the laws that forced the separation of banks and securities firms.

Goldman was behind in other trends on Wall Street. Despite concerted efforts to compete, the firm was far behind the leader Salomon Brothers in the growing area of mortgage-backed securities. In 1986, Goldman had less than one-sixth the public mortgage-backed underwriting volume of Salomon and less than five percent of this market.

There were more problems. Goldman had been slow to enter growing international markets. A recently acquired commodities firm had been floundering. Some of the top commercial-paper clients no longer needed Goldman, as many large companies could issue such paper on their own. The head of the firm's takeover-stock arbitrage unit would soon face allegations of insider trading.

While all this was going on, Drexel was becoming a major investment banker. In 1986, the upstart firm of Drexel Burnham achieved revenues of more than $4 billion and profits of $545 million.

If Goldman were to be a dominant competitor in the leverage world of the 1980s, an original tactic would be most useful. But it had to be a tactic that turned the game around, one that gave the client-friendly advisor the advantage over the takeover player, one that was based on Goldman's strengths rather than Drexel's. During 1985 and 1986, such tactic took shape.

Part II.
THE ANSWER

5. The Public LBO

What vulnerable companies needed was a new maneuver to counter Drexel-financed takeover players, who currently had all the advantage. There were several criteria for this tactic.

First, it should be a tactic that provided defense protection. Such protection should, ideally, be achieved in a positive manner. Although new defense tactics such as "poison pills" (discussed later) were becoming popular, most of these accomplished their purpose by simply inhibiting outside offers. A better tactic would be one that accomplished its defense purpose while also rewarding shareholders.

The tactic should transfer the advantage from the takeover player to management. It should give a management the ability to make a preemptive move, preferably without putting the company "in play" (i.e., in a state of frenzied stock trading or imminent takeover peril), where there was the risk of losing a bidding war. Most important, the tactic should possess some feature that provided a *value edge* over competing offers—but an advantage that the takeover players couldn't easily duplicate. This value edge had to be based on a solid financial premise, not a one-shot legal ploy, in order that directors could

58 THE ANSWER

approve the solution without worrying about shareholder lawsuits or about the tactic being overturned in court. The tactic would also have to be relatively easy to finance—at least on a competitive basis with Drexel.

But in order to convince executives to attempt such a maneuver, it wouldn't be enough to just promise that they would keep their jobs. The tactic should also give some incentives to management. Ideally, these would be in the form of LBO-type equity returns and/or the cashing out of management stockholdings at a sizeable premium. Of course, from the investment banker's perspective, the tactic should include enough debt to require mezzanine financing, thereby providing large fees.

The criteria for the ultimate leverage/defense tactic were clear. In the heat of another LBO battle, the answer appeared.

At the end of 1984, Multimedia Inc. (not to be confused with John Kluge's *Metro*media) was a powerful communications company based in Greenville, South Carolina. The firm published newspapers and owned and operated radio and television stations. It also syndicated several popular television programs, including those of Phil Donahue and Sally Jessy Raphael. What's more, Multimedia had some fast-growing operations in cable TV.

With their predictable cash flows and easy-to-divest operations, communications companies such as Multimedia were the current darlings of the LBO crowd. (Besides the Metromedia deal, leveraged buyouts had recently been done at Harte-Hanks Communications and Wometco Enterprises, and would soon be done with Storer Communications.) Multimedia itself had grown rapidly, its revenues and operating profits having doubled over the last five years.

Multimedia's stock was trading around $35, which meant the firm was valued at about six-times its cash flow, a reasonable multiple for a normal company. But given the growth potential of some of its operations, Multimedia was, in fact, underpriced by the market. This firm was a candidate for an LBO.

There were a couple other aspects of Multimedia that provided good LBO potential. About 40 percent of the stock was owned by members of the founding families of the company and certain members of senior management, *and* under South Carolina law, a merger by the firm would require the approval of at least two-thirds of the shareholders. Consequently, any outside bidder for Multimedia would be blocked as long as the founding-families and management shareholders stuck together. Also, since Multimedia owned television and radio stations, a sale of the company would have to be approved by the Federal Communications Commission (FCC).

Thus, if the management and founding-families shareholders were to attempt a leveraged buyout of this firm, the deal would seem to be immune from interference by outside suitors—and thereby assured of victory.

In early 1985, an investor group led by certain members of senior management and including members of the founding families, such group being advised by Goldman Sachs, announced a plan to purchase the outstanding shares of Multimedia in an LBO. The offer consisted of $37-per-share in cash and $25-per-share in face value of securities, in the form of discount debentures. The value of the securities was estimated at about $12.50 per share, making the buyout group's bid worth roughly $49.50 per share.

A committee of independent directors was set up by the Multimedia board to review the fairness of the offer. Then a huge surprise arrived. Wesray (former Treasury Secretary William Simon's investment firm) reportedly came to Multimedia with a $60-per-share offer.

The buyout group now had a problem. Wesray was in no way a greenmailer; Simon had a proven record of completing leveraged deals. With a legitimate LBO player making a bid 20 percent higher than its own, the buyout group would need to significantly sweeten its offer.[*]

However, increasing the bid would require raising more financing. Of course, the offer could be sweetened by increasing the face value

---

[*] It should be noted that although this bid was widely rumored to be a $60-per-share offer from Wesray, to the author's knowledge neither the amount nor the source of the bid was ever publicly confirmed by Multimedia or Wesray.

60 THE ANSWER

of the discount debentures. But such a payment might not be competitive in the eyes of the fairness committee with a $60-per-share cash offer from a genuine player. With Multimedia's stock price having risen above the buyout group's bid, a comeback was needed fast.

What would be useful for the Multimedia buyout group would be some sort of new twist, an innovative plan that would outdo the $60-per-share offer without requiring a large amount of additional financing. In fact, what would be really great would be a plan that would endear outside shareholders.

How might that be done? Some bright minds at Goldman and the law firm of Wachtell Lipton came up with a clever plan. The new plan would give the outside shareholders the chance to get a piece of the equity of the newly leveraged Multimedia—and thereby get in on those LBO returns.

The new plan was soon announced. The outside stockholders would receive $41.25-per-share of cash, plus securities with an estimated value of about $13 per share, for a total package of roughly $54 per share. This was still much less than the reported $60-per-share offer. However, the Multimedia group's new plan had an additional critical feature: The offer would allow shareholders to elect to take one-half of a share of post-buyout stock (for each share they currently owned) in place of $5.25 of the cash distribution.

What exactly was this new plan? It was sort of an LBO, in that the shareholders were being bought out in a deal financed with debt. But the plan was also sort of just a refinancing of Multimedia. That was because many of the current shareholders would elect to take the new half-shares and thus continue to own stock in the company, and the new shares would still be publicly traded.

Sort of an LBO and sort of a refinancing. Wall Street was having trouble defining the genus of this hybrid animal. The plan was simply termed a "recapitalization."

The Multimedia board of directors approved the recapitalization. This, of course, brings up an obvious question: How can $54 per share be considered competitive with $60?

One factor was the half-shares of post-recapitalization stock that the shareholders were getting a shot at. Even though the new plan was $6 per share less than a $60 offer, a stockholder might come out ahead by choosing to take the new half-shares. That was because he would then receive an opportunity at the future value growth of that equity.

With Multimedia having good LBO traits and taking on high leverage in the deal, the company's post-recapitalization stock should act like LBO equity. Such shares would therefore have the chance for huge price appreciation. The new half-shares were a type of *value wildcard*, the value edge that was crucial to the ultimate leverage/defense tactic. The plan had the potential to be worth more than $60 per share to the current stockholders.

It should be mentioned that there had been other recapitalization plans. The most notable was the one announced by Phillips Petroleum (advised by Morgan Stanley and First Boston) in late 1984 in response to Boone Pickens.

But in these earlier cases, the recapitalization had been presented in a different way. In previous cases, this tactic appeared as mainly the act of taking on massive debt to make a repurchase of shares. In the process, companies had appeared to be uglifying themselves with debt in order to avoid takeover threats.

The plan for Multimedia, on the other hand, put a different face on the recapitalization concept. This was not simply a plan to take on debt to buy back shares. Instead, Multimedia was making a value distribution, plus granting "new" equity. The recapitalization was a fresh idea that was giving the shareholders a way into an LBO.

Despite the clever recapitalization plan, it turned out that the battle for Multimedia was far from over. Shortly after the plan was approved, Lorimar Inc.—creator of the *Falcon Crest*, *Knots Landing*, and *Dallas* television shows—made a $61-per-share proposal. What's more, Lorimar was using an investment banker by the name of Drexel Burnham.

How did Multimedia react to Lorimar's offer? Actually, it stated that *the company was not for sale.*

Not for sale??? How could this be?

This was where another important aspect of the plan came in. While some stockholders would be completely bought out, every outside holder had the chance to take the half-shares and remain a stockholder—and many would.

Thus the plan was not a complete buyout. While the percentage-ownership profile would change somewhat, the shareholder composition would, to a large extent, remain the same. The company was not really being bought out. It was simply "recapitalizing."

Lorimar bowed out soon after making its offer, and the affair would have been finished except that Jack Kent Cooke—owner of the *Washington Redskins* football team—had entered the game. Cooke had received a taste of the pleasures of communications LBOs when he was allowed to invest in the equity of the Metromedia buyout. Now he proposed a $63-per-share deal for Multimedia. When his idea failed to elicit a positive response, Cooke raised the price to $65 per share.

With such a rich proposal on the table, the founding-families shareholders were increasingly under pressure to break rank. However, Multimedia's board soon rejected the $65-per-share deal, and the recapitalization plan received FCC approval.

Cooke now played his trump card by announcing a two-step tender offer. Cooke said he would offer $70-per-share in cash for 40 percent of Multimedia's shares. (When combined with a stake he already held, this would give him more than 50 percent of the company.) If enough shares were tendered to finish Step One, he would then offer $70-per-share in a combination of cash and securities for the remaining shares.

Cooke's offer was really putting pressure on the founding-families shareholders. Those who tendered might realize $70-per-share in cash, while those who didn't could end up with securities from a seemingly high-priced deal. After all, $70 per share was an incredibly rich 12-times Multimedia's cash flow. Even with the company's growth potential, could the debt from such a deal be serviced?

Sticking with the recapitalization would be a real gamble for shareholders. Would the plan hold up? The time when Cooke was to file his tender offer with the SEC approached.

It would have been risky to call Cooke's bluff. If he actually started the tender offer, all hell might break loose. A few hours before Cooke was to file his tender offer, his holdings were agreed to be bought back at $70 per share.

Many of the outside shareholders were less than thrilled about Cooke being bought out by Multimedia at $70—and thus losing their own chance at getting that amount from him. If the recapitalization tactic were to gain favor, it would be helpful if the shares of Multimedia would increase in value very quickly.

Things couldn't have worked out better. The Multimedia stock traded at $19 right after the recapitalization, which was almost twice the $10.50 implicitly estimated value of the shares. (Remember that a half-share was given in place of $5.25 of cash.) Two months after the deal, the stock was above $30. Six months later, the shares hit $43! The stockholders who had taken the half-shares had a value package that was worth nearly twice what Multimedia had been trading at before the LBO idea surfaced.

It seemed the recapitalization had produced a miracle. Those stockholders who chose the new shares achieved LBO-type returns right away, and with a publicly traded security. Relative to the $10.50 implicit valuation, the new shares had achieved a *300 percent* return in less than a year!

The ideal tactic had been found. The "leveraged recapitalization," or "recap," as the tactic would come to be known, was the ultimate leverage/defense tool.

All the elements were here. The recapitalization gave the advantage to management. The new shares provided a value wildcard that produced a distinct edge.

64 THE ANSWER

The tactic provided defense protection by greatly increasing the company's debt load. This was accomplished while also rewarding shareholders, through both a large immediate payment and a chance at LBO-type equity returns. And for future cases, the performance of Multimedia's stock was proof of the enormous return potential on recapitalization equity.

The tactic could be implemented before a takeover player appeared—and since it was not a sale of the company, would not create a state of bidding. The recapitalization was based on solid financial footing. Furthermore, the concept had an air of fealty: a recapitalization kept the company "independent," with the basic shareholder make-up intact.

The Multimedia plan gave incentives to senior management in the form of the cash-out of existing holdings plus LBO returns on new equity. Most important for the investment-banker advisor, the recap tactic provided a leveraged-deal financing opportunity and the accompanying fees.

However, there were aspects of the Multimedia deal that might not reoccur. A large shareholder had been bought out in this affair. In future recaps, would the other shareholders tolerate such an action? And there certainly wouldn't be many deals where a friendly group owned 40 percent of the equity before the affair began. Would the leveraged-recapitalization tactic stand up?

Some fine-tuning could be required, but at last Goldman had ammunition in its arsenal. Soon a full-scale firing would occur.

The era of the leveraged recapitalization officially began on February 22, 1986. That's when FMC Corporation—a Chicago-based producer of machinery and chemicals—announced its version of this tactic.

The structure of the FMC recap was somewhat different from Multimedia's. Under the FMC plan, there were no choices for outside shareholders; they all were to receive a $70-per-share cash distribution and one new share of stock for each old share they held. To finance the cash payment, FMC would borrow $1.3 billion in bank loans, plus $400 million in subordinated debt to be arranged by Goldman Sachs.

The FMC plan had an original aspect for the treatment of certain shareholdings; specifically, the shareholdings of certain members of management and certain employee-benefit plans. These shareholders would not receive the $70 cash payment. Instead, they would have each share they currently held "rolled over" (i.e., converted) into a multiple of new shares.

What was the purpose of this rollover of shares? One function was additional defense protection. By converting executive and employee-benefit-plan shares into more shares, the amount of stock in the hands of voting groups friendly to the company would be greatly increased—from about 18 percent of all pre-recap shares to more than 35 percent post-recap. With so much stock under employee control and a heavy debt load, it would be unlikely that anyone would make a hostile move at FMC.

Another reason for the rollover involved taxes. In order for the outside shareholders to receive capital-gains treatment on their recap cash distribution (there was such a thing as preferential capital-gains treatment back in 1986), they had to have their post-recap ownership interest reduced to less than 80 percent of their pre-recap interest. By increasing the number of shares held by various employee stockholders, the rollover accomplished this.

However, there was another aspect of the rollover that had nothing to do with tax or defense issues. As we'll see, the rollover would create a marvelous wealth opportunity.

The basic rollover ratio was 5.67 new shares for each old share. How was this ratio arrived at? The rollover ratio was based on the expected value of a new share of stock after the recap. A ratio of 5.67 new shares for each old share meant that the value of the post-recap stock was being estimated at about $15 per share, as $15 for a new share plus $70 of cash (given in exchange for an old share) is $85, and $85 divided by $15 equals 5.67.

66 THE ANSWER

This was a bit confusing. But what would turn out to be really great for the shareholders getting the rollover would be if the new shares would quickly go up in price. Given that FMC's stock price had risen from about $85 at the time the recap was announced to $92 by early April, it seemed there was a good chance this would be the case. There were, however, some other parties that were beginning to figure this out. One of these was legendary arbitrageur Ivan Boesky.

Boesky, who had purchased a holding of FMC shares, argued that with the stock now trading at more than $85, those shareholders who were receiving a rollover were getting a better deal than the outside shareholders. So he threatened to vote against the plan.

Since a significant portion of FMC's stock was now in the hands of arbs, Boesky's contention imperiled a favorable shareholder vote. FMC soon sweetened the cash distribution to the outside stockholders to $80 per share.

FMC's stock price kept on rising to $100. Having obtained a good return on his shares, Boesky sold off much of his stake. There were no further disturbances, the recap financing was eventually completed, and the plan was approved by the shareholders.

After the $80-per-share cash payment, the new FMC shares began trading at $19.[*] And just as in the case of Multimedia, these shares soon rose dramatically in price. In February 1987, FMC's stock hit $33. The price then continued to ascend during the following eight months, eventually reaching $60.

This was a bonanza for the shareholders. For outside shareholders, the $60 stock price meant they had obtained $140 of value for each old share ($80 of cash plus one new share at $60 equals $140), a healthy 65 percent pre-tax gain over the $85 pre-recap-announcement price.

The shareholders who received the 5.67 rollover did even better. They obtained $340 of value per old share (5.67 new shares x $60 = $340). This was *4-times* what the stock had been trading at when the

---

[*] As with a dividend or any monetary distribution to shareholders, the per-share payment made in a recapitalization causes the stock price to decline by a like amount.

recap idea was announced. In other words, a 300 percent return in less than two years!

With the success of the FMC recap, it suddenly became apparent to nervous executives that it paid to have friends at Goldman. It also paid for an investment-banking firm to have clients who were willing to try the new leverage tactic: Goldman's fees in the FMC recap were at least $17 million.

The new tool had begun to be perfected. At FMC, the recap tactic again produced large benefits to the shareholders, providing both an immediate cash payment and the fulfillment of LBO-type equity returns. The plan provided defense protection through a combination of high debt and greatly increased employee ownership. The FMC case also proved that a recap could be accomplished proactively while not eliciting any outside offers (despite the annoyance of Boesky), all without officially putting the company up for bid.

With the FMC triumph, the recap had been established as a preemptive leverage/defense measure, the answer that corporate executives were waiting for. Goldman was back in the saddle. The firm possessed a weapon that allowed it to strongly compete in the leverage game.

It should be noted that, like LBOs, leveraged recapitalizations had previously been done, especially at small, privately held firms. For example, a business owner might want to take cash out of his company—such as to pay for the kids' college tuition—without having to sell part or all of the firm. To do this, the owner could simply "recapitalize" the company with debt, borrowing against the assets of the business and distributing the proceeds to himself. The newly added debt would then be serviced by future cash flows.[*]

---

[*] Leveraged recapitalizations were sometimes referred to as leveraged "cash-outs." Also, the term "recapitalization" can refer to any significant change in the capital structure of a company. Prior to (and subsequent to) the debt-crazed 1980s, recapitalizations of large companies typically were financial restructurings that reduced the debt and increased the equity of an overleveraged or bankrupt firm.

In regard to the recapitalization of a publicly traded company, one might ask why loading up on debt would provide defense protection? Couldn't a takeover player just buy up the post-recap stock—which would be easy to do given the initially low price of the shares—and then assume or refinance the debt?

Theoretically, this could be done. However, the provisions of leveraged-deal debt usually are quite onerous. The terms of such instruments generally require immediate repayment in the event of a "change in control" of the ownership of the company, which is usually defined as a 20 percent equity stake being accumulated by a single party. In addition, the debt often has "poison" provisions that require large premiums to be paid in refinancing if the change-in-control threshold is crossed. Trying to take over a recapitalized company would be messy and expensive.

One might ask why the management of a public company would want to do a recap as a proactive measure? Why not just hook up with an LBO firm and attempt a leveraged buyout, where, if successful, management would get a large equity position and the opportunity to achieve high returns. Wouldn't it be less desirable to manage a recapitalized company—which still has the scrutiny of public shareholders—than to run a firm that has gone "private" in an LBO?

It turns out that a major reason the recap tactic was preferable to an LBO as a proactive measure was because of a legal point. You see, a leveraged buyout involves the sale of the company; whereas a recap, as alluded to earlier, doesn't. And because an LBO is a sale, the company's board of directors is under a duty to obtain the highest possible price for the firm. Thus a board-of-directors' responsibilities in an LBO includes the solicitation of competing bids in order to assure that outside shareholders are treated fairly. This creates the possibility that management might end up in a bidding war.

Hence, an LBO was a risky maneuver, as management had no guaranteed advantage over outsiders. Once a company's executives proposed such a plan, they theoretically became just another bidder in a battle that could get very messy, very fast (witness National Gypsum). On the other hand, since a recap is not a sale of the company, the board of directors is under no duty to seek competing offers. The company is simply borrowing some money (albeit a huge amount) and distributing it to the shareholders.

As a result, the recap gave management a clear advantage. And there was a further possible benefit of the "not a sale" aspect. Although the concept hadn't been conclusively proven, it presumably could be argued that a recap plan wouldn't even have to be compared to outside bids.

There was another potential aspect of the recap that could make it the tactic of choice. The recaps Goldman had advised on so far had required the approval of the shareholders through a special vote. But as was evident from the National Gypsum LBO, a shareholder vote creates risk, for it allows time for outside offers to appear. Yet if necessary for the sake of speed, the approval of a recap plan theoretically could be granted *merely by a vote of the board of directors*.

Thus the recap appeared to be the perfect proactive leverage/defense tool. A management could attempt such a plan under the logic of maximizing shareholder value, then protect the company through the "not a sale" aspect if outside bids should appear. What's more, even if an attractive offer did surface, a recap could compete very well with such a bid. The following example is provided to illustrate this point.

Assume there is a company that proposed a recap plan which would give each current stockholder a $45 cash distribution plus a new share of stock in exchange for each existing share. An outsider then bids $50 per share for the company, the outsider arguing that his offer is superior in value to the recap.

Obviously, the superiority of the outside bid versus the recap depends on the value of the new shares of stock (following the cash distribution)—which in recaps eventually came to be known as "stub" shares (as only a "stub" of equity value was left after the distribution). In this example, if the value of a stub share is more than $5, the recap is clearly better.

However, prior to the cash distribution, the stock is not yet trading as a post-recap stub. In order to compare the value of the recap to the outside bid, the expected trading price of the stub shares must be estimated.* **

Hence, the company doing the recap could claim value superiority over the outside bidder on the basis of the stub assessment. Furthermore, even if the cash distribution plus the estimated value of the stub was *less* than the outside bid, a case could still be made that the recap was better. That's because (as was noted in the discussion of Multimedia) the stub shares will give the stockholder the *potential* for huge future returns. Since the company will be highly leveraged after the recap, the stub should act just like equity in an LBO, with any change in the value of the firm being magnified in the value of the stub.

To show how the stub value would fluctuate, assume that the hypothetical company doing the recap had cash flow of $10 per share. Using a conservative valuation multiple of 5-times cash flow, the company would be worth $10 cash flow x 5 multiple = $50 per share. Further assume that the company had no debt before the recap, and thus the pre-recap equity was also worth $50 per share.

After the $45-per-share cash distribution was made (and assume was financed entirely with debt), the stub equity would be worth $5 per share. This is calculated as the $50-per-share value of the cash flow minus the $45-per-share of debt.

But keep one thing in mind. Even though the company's equity is now worth just $5 per share, it is only the financial structure of the firm that has changed as a result of the recap—*not the cash flow or total value of that flow.* The total value of the company is still $50 per share. The capitalization of the firm is now made up of $45-per-share of debt (which is being serviced by the cash flow) and $5-per-share left over in equity, which sum to $50.

---

*In some cases, stub shares were traded on a "when issued" basis prior to the completion of the recap.

**The analysis for a stub-share valuation estimate in a recap was typically done by the investment-banker advisor. However, such estimate was officially and ultimately the conclusion of the company undergoing the recap based on "consultation with" the investment banker.

Now assume that the cash flow increases by 20 percent, to $12 per share. The total value of the company would also go up by 20 percent, from the original $50 per share to $60 per share (calculated as $12 cash flow x 5 multiple = $60 per share). Subtracting the debt from $60-per-share of total value results in a stub value of $15 per share. The stub has gone from $5 to $15, *a 200 percent increase*, even though cash flow increased by only 20 percent. Such is the power of leverage.

In selling a recap plan to a board of directors, projections would be given showing post-recap cost savings and improvements in operations that would boost future cash flow. The forecasted increase in cash flow would then be predicted to cause the stub to exhibit the type of value growth described above. Given this aspect, it could be implied that the recap plan would provide even more value than outside offers higher than $50 per share.

There was another reason that corporate executives would prefer a recap over an LBO. This aspect had to do with the measure of control that management would maintain.

When management joins forces with an LBO firm, the people who bring the money get to make the rules. Management is generally allowed to purchase only 10 percent to 20 percent of the LBO equity (the rest going to the LBO organizers and to those providing mezzanine financing). The company usually gets a whole new board of directors that is controlled by the LBO firm. The company executives are retained mainly to keep the cash flow coming. All the real power and final authority rests with the LBO-firm principals.

In a recap, however, management keeps its executive authority. And management's jobs are even further secured as a result of the large debt and increase in friendly stock ownership.

Another factor is liquidity. In an LBO, there is no immediate liquidity for one's equity. Once an executive sinks money into the deal, there isn't a ready market in which to sell his holdings.

On the other hand, recap stub shares could be bought and sold at one's pleasure in the most liquid of public markets. Indeed, a recap provided the best of all worlds to both corporate managements and shareholders. This tactic gave everyone the chance to get in on the favorable aspects of leverage simply by holding stock in a publicly traded company. In fact, the leveraged recapitalization soon came to be known as "The Public LBO."

Shortly after the FMC deal, another recap opportunity arose for Goldman. Owens-Corning (the fiberglass company) was in need of defense assistance.

During the summer of 1986, some unusual trading activity occurred in the shares of Owens-Corning. The stock price, which had been in the high $30s earlier in the year, hovered around $50 during the first three weeks of July. Then near the end of July, Owens-Corning shares began to experience heavy trading volume, with the price eventually rising above $70.

On August 5, Sanford Sigoloff telephoned the CEO of Owens-Corning. The purpose of the call was to request a meeting to discuss a possible merger between Wickes and Owens-Corning. Mr. Sigoloff stated that if his request for a meeting were refused, Wickes would immediately begin a tender offer. He further stated that Wickes owned approximately 8 percent to 10 percent of Owens-Corning's shares.

The Owens-Corning CEO met with Sigoloff on August 11. The CEO indicated that Owens-Corning wasn't interested in pursuing a merger with Wickes, and stated that Owens-Corning was considering a restructuring plan. Shortly thereafter, Wickes began a tender offer at a price of $74 per share.

The Owens-Corning board of directors met on August 21 and determined the Wickes offer to be inadequate and not in the best interests of the company, and recommended that the shareholders not tender to it. The board then resolved that—with the advice of Goldman Sachs—alternative transactions be investigated, including an LBO, a merger with another company, and a leveraged recapitalization.

The Owens-Corning case provided a great opportunity. Here was the chance to conclusively prove the recap as an alternative to an announced bid by a Drexel-financed player. Such a success could cement Goldman's stature as the premier defender.

Although several potential white knights and LBO firms were contacted, none of them panned out. At a board meeting on August 28, a recap proposal was presented. The Owens-Corning plan called for the distribution of $52-per-share in cash, plus $35-per-share of face value of discount debentures.*

Was the recap plan worth more than Wickes' $74-per-share offer? The discount debentures were figured to be worth about $16 per share, making the cash-plus-debt distribution worth about $68 per share. Hence, the key to the competitiveness of the recap was the value of a stub share, which was estimated to be in the range of $12 to $18. In other words, the plan would provide somewhere between $80 and $86 per share, and $83 if one took the midpoint.

The Owens-Corning board approved the proposal on August 28. A recap now had the chance to subdue a Drexel-financed foe.

And it worked. The day after the Owens-Corning board approved the recap, Wickes dropped the tender offer and began to sell its stake.

With the Owens-Corning deal, the recap had been solidified as a viable tactic in the face of an outside offer. Unfortunately, as fast as Goldman could establish the tactic, there was competition.

In the FMC recap, Morgan Stanley had been retained to provide an opinion on the fairness of the plan to shareholders. What's more, there was already some knowledge of recaps at Morgan Stanley, the firm having advised on the Phillips Petroleum plan. Thus it was not a surprise when, in July 1986, Colt Industries announced a plan for a $1.5 billion recap advised on by Morgan Stanley. Many of the features of the Colt Industries recap were similar to the FMC deal, with employee holdings increasing from less than 10 percent to more than 30 percent through rollovers.

---

* It wasn't surprising that Owens-Corning's management would attempt a recap. The CEO was a director of a company known by the initials "FMC."

There was, however, some good news for Goldman in the Colt Industries recap. Even though this company wasn't under immediate takeover pressure, the plan was easily approved. It was thereby established that a recap could be done entirely on the basis of value creation.

Yet the Colt Industries deal was also somewhat disconcerting. That was because a firm named Drexel Burnham was used to help raise part of the financing.

6. Goldman Saki

It seemed as if the recap might be the ultimate defense tool. Perhaps this tactic was invincible. Then again, the inability to arrange instant financing in the manner of Drexel remained an issue. What would happen if a Drexel client who was intent on actually purchasing the target company came full force against the recap tactic?

At the same time the FMC recap was in progress, Goldman found out what would happen. The case of Warnaco was the showdown.

In 1985, Warnaco Inc. was a clothing manufacturer based in Bridgeport, Connecticut. The company's products were sold under a number of popular labels, including Hathaway shirts, Dior, Chaps, Speedo, White Stag, and Geoffrey Beene. These were all names with consumer loyalty that could produce cash flow or be expanded upon. With the market valuing the firm at four-times cash flow, Warnaco was a candidate for leverage.

In early 1985, certain top executives and directors of Warnaco began a strategic review of the company, which included discussions with representatives of Goldman Sachs. This was before the recap tactic had been popularized, and thus the LBO was the leverage tactic of choice at the time. In October of 1985, a group of Warnaco senior executives made an LBO proposal.

The proposal was for $27-per-share in cash and $13-per-share in face value of discount debentures. The debentures were figured to be worth about $6 per share, giving the package a value of roughly $33 per share.

To provide funding, Goldman utilized a source from the Macy's deal, GE Credit. GE Credit soon gave a financing-commitment letter. The Warnaco board of directors approved the LBO in December 1985. There would be four months to finalize things prior to a scheduled shareholder meeting to vote on the plan.

There was, however, one problem with this plan. The Warnaco executives and their advisor hadn't been totally original in coming up with the LBO idea.

Back in January 1985, Warnaco's CEO had been approached about doing a leveraged buyout with a group headed by investor Andrew Galef. Such group also included a former executive of a Warnaco division. The CEO had told the Galef group he had no interest in doing an LBO with them.

The Galef group didn't reappear during the time when the Warnaco buyout group was presenting its offer to the board, or in the three months after board approval. However, one month before the scheduled shareholder vote on the LBO, the Galef group did reappear. Using an acquisition vehicle titled W Acquisition ("WA"), the investor group suddenly announced a tender offer for Warnaco's shares. The price was $36 per share—all in cash. WA also said it possessed the "highly confident" backing of Drexel Burnham.

At this point in time, it would have been difficult to go LBO versus LBO with a Drexel client. What would be useful would be a tactic that could compete against WA's financing strength. Given the recent success of Multimedia, now was the chance to truly prove the recap tactic as a defensive tool in a heated battle.

Four days after the tender offer began, Warnaco's board held a meeting at which a recap plan was presented. The Warnaco recap would pay a combination of cash, debt, and a stub share, the sum of which was expected to be worth more than $36 per share. However, the exact structure of the payment was somewhat unusual.

The LBO funding was now out. With only a month to go before the shareholders would be asked to vote on the proposed recap (and a hostile tender offer in effect), there was little time to arrange a whole new funding group. As a result, cram-down financing would *really* be put to the test in this proposal. In the Warnaco recap distribution, only $7 per share would be in cash. Other than the stub, the rest of the distribution would consist *entirely of subordinated notes and debentures*.

Furthermore, the plan would pay out more cash (in lieu of the securities), *if* Goldman could place the subordinated notes with outside investors. But such placement was in no way guaranteed.

In other words, Warnaco's stockholders themselves would likely be providing most of the financing for the recap. One thing was for sure: If this plan worked, it would prove forever that the recap tactic could prevail with cram-down financing.

Warnaco's board approved the plan two days after it was presented. Goldman had 33 days (prior to a shareholder vote on the plan) to arrange financing in order to increase the cash portion of the distribution.

Unlike the Owens-Corning affair, which ended upon board approval of the recap, the Warnaco battle was far from over. WA soon raised its offer to $40 per share.

The issue for the shareholders was which side was providing greater value. Although no official estimate had been made of the stub-share value, a value had been implied in that some post-recap equity was being offered to institutional lenders at a $5-per-share price. Thus the Warnaco recap distribution ostensibly was worth about $39 per share.

WA soon upped its price, announcing it would be willing to pay $42.50 per share if the Warnaco board agreed to the deal.

In response, the cash portion of the recap distribution was increased, but by only $2 (to a total of $9 per share). The face value of the debt was increased by $1 per share.

WA went to $44 per share. Warnaco countered by announcing that Goldman had placed the subordinated notes. The recap cash payment was now $25 per share.

WA raised its price again, to $46.50 per share. Warnaco's shareholders tendered en masse. With more than 50 percent of the shares in WA's hands, the Warnaco board accepted the offer. It was over. Drexel's client had prevailed.

It could be claimed that the best price had been achieved for the shareholders. Nevertheless, the Warnaco affair was a defeat for Goldman and the recap tactic. In the final analysis, in a head-to-head competition against a Drexel-financed foe that was determined to acquire the target company, the new defense tool had lost. Without the financing strength to back it up, the recap could not be considered an invincible tactic.

The Warnaco conflict had crystallized Goldman's weakness versus Drexel. Even though a significant amount of the recap funding had eventually been placed, it wasn't enough against a persistent Drexel-financed opponent. Raising subordinated debt through the normal channels took too long, and one couldn't rely on tactics such as cram-down debt. For the recap tactic to be effective against any opponent, there had to be a large and reliable source of quick mezzanine financing.*

---

* Technically, the subordinated debt in a recap wasn't "mezzanine" debt as such, since there usually wasn't a layer of equity being financed. However, the term *mezzanine financing* will be used interchangeably with subordinated financing in regard to recaps.

In 1986, junk bonds commanded the world of finance. The victory at Warnaco was just one illustration of this instrument's power. Milken's system was dominating.

Yet despite having been used to fund several large deals, junk financing needed a showcase deal, a definitive conquest that would prove such instrument could facilitate virtually any transaction no matter the size.

With Beatrice, it happened. In late 1985, KKR convinced the board of Beatrice, a food/consumer-products company, to approve a buyout. The Beatrice LBO would be an incredible $6.2 billion leveraged deal that could show that junk financing worked in the most massive of transactions. And it did. Through the $2.5 billion of junk funding that Drexel arranged, the huge Beatrice LBO was completed—and became the showcase deal that proved testament to the ultimate financing ability of Drexel.

The Beatrice LBO (and subsequent refinancings and divestitures) was a fees orgy. In all, the commercial bankers, lawyers, investment bankers, and KKR garnered more than $250 million of fees. But Drexel, by far, obtained the most. Counting the firm's work for selling junk securities, refinancing debt, and advising on divestitures (some of which were also LBOs), Drexel reaped more than $170 million.

An even bigger reward came from equity warrants. Junk financing was so important in the Beatrice LBO that Drexel was able to obtain a large amount of equity—both in the original deal and in companies that were divested. After KKR quickly sold off numerous Beatrice operations at high prices, the equity interests held by Drexel and its employees were estimated to be worth in excess of *$600 million.*

The Beatrice LBO was a landmark. It proved that virtually no leveraged deal was too large or too complicated. And it showed how such a transaction could produce mind-numbing riches.

But if any firm other than Drexel hoped to play in the mega-LBO game, it would need to create a method of real-time financing that replicated the effect of Milken's system. Not that there weren't minds trying to find an answer to this puzzle. In 1986, an apparent solution emerged. It was at this point that the top investment-banking firms followed divergent paths in leveraged-deal financing—First Boston, Shearson Lehman, Merrill Lynch, and Morgan Stanley taking one direction, and Goldman another.

The quickest way for an investment-banking firm to raise financing is to simply lend its own money. For example, when a company plans to issue securities, it sometimes can't wait to get the money. The company may have to be advanced funds in what is known as a "bridge loan," which "bridges" the financing while the underwriter prepares the offering.

The situation in leveraged deals was similar to that of a company which required a bridge loan. A deal might be all set up, but the acquirer couldn't wait for the investment banker to place all the mezzanine financing, as any delay might allow a Drexel client to come in and grab the target. What such acquirers needed was a bridge loan for the mezzanine debt.

By 1986, most of the major investment-banking houses had more than a billion dollars of capital, plus large debt capacity. What's more, most were now public companies, with outside shareholders' money to utilize.

Hence, if an acquirer needed a few hundred-million dollars for a short-term loan to complete a deal, the investment banker could simply advance its own funds. Once the acquisition was completed, the investment banker could then set about the task of arranging permanent financing for the client to replace the bridge loan. In late 1986, First Boston used this very technique to finance the final $800 million in Campeau Corporation's purchase of Allied Stores—and thus the "bridge loan" was born in leveraged deals.

Bridge debt also provided an extra benefit for the investment banker. When the bridge-loan technique was used in a leveraged deal, the mezzanine financing was done twice: once for the quick bridge loan to get the deal done, and again later to replace the loan with permanent debt. And even though the bridge loan might be outstanding for only a couple of months, the investment banker charged the client a fee for both financings. Bridge debt produced double fees.

However, using bridge debt in a leveraged deal caused a risk problem for the investment banker. For example, what if the market for junk debt or the fortunes of the acquired company changed dramatically after the deal? What if divestitures couldn't be made at the predicted values? What if the deal was overpriced to begin with? The investment banker could then be stuck holding bridge debt that couldn't be refinanced and/or the client might have difficulty making payments on.

This could be a problem. Yet in the atmosphere of 1986, it didn't seem so. The junk-bond and M&A markets were booming. The economy was growing. It didn't seem there would be any problem refinancing a bridge loan.

Bridge debt could have been an answer for Goldman. However, Goldman was still a partnership. If a large bridge loan went bad, it could wipe out a huge chunk of the partners' equity capital. Bridge loans seemed better suited to the investment-banking firms that were now public companies (such as Merrill Lynch, First Boston, Morgan Stanley, Shearson Lehman, and Salomon), which could employ their shareholders' money.

Instead of putting up the partners' money or slugging it out in the domestic junk market against Drexel, it would be preferable for Goldman to have its own source where it could instantly place mezzanine debt among eager purchasers. The firm had a number of reliable purchasers from the leveraged deals it had already done, but needed more to have a truly competitive system.

A break in this regard came in August 1986, when Goldman created a link with Sumitomo Bank Ltd., the third-largest bank in the world. The Japanese firm would become a limited partner in Goldman Sachs in exchange for a $500 million investment. Goldman chairman John Weinberg stated that the investment would "assist Goldman Sachs in meeting capital requirements for our rapidly growing worldwide businesses."

It should be noted that capital is critical for an investment-banking firm, and Goldman could use all the capital it could get. But capital wasn't the only benefit of this deal. An important benefit of the alliance was increased access to eager investors throughout Japan.

The Japanese were loaded with cash and in love with American securities and assets. Japanese banks and investors would soon be fighting over American leveraged-deal debt.

Goldman would create numerous financing contacts in Japan. These investors would then provide a source that could purchase recap mezzanine debt quickly, providing time until the debt could be replaced (for a second fee) in the American markets. When combined with Goldman's U.S. sources, these purchasers would provide a reliable source of real-time mezzanine funding. And it would be done without risking Goldman's own capital.

7. The Bridge Game

There was a rush to get deals done by the end of 1986, for at December 31, new tax laws would go into effect. Among many revisions, the new laws would effectively reduce the depreciation write-offs available for acquired assets, thereby making acquisitions more costly. The flurry of activity sent the dollar volume of M&A transactions to a record level in the fourth quarter.

The leverage game suffered a blow in November 1986 when news of the Ivan Boesky investigation broke. The famous arbitrageur admitted to insider trading, and agreed to pay a $100 million penalty and plead guilty to a criminal charge. Upon the announcement of Boesky's agreement, the junk-bond market went into a state of unrest, as it was revealed that Drexel was under SEC investigation.

It seemed the LBO and takeover boom would be dampened until the loopholes in the new tax laws had been ferreted out and the junk-bond market had recovered from the Boesky news. But then a strange thing happened. After a brief respite in the first quarter of 1987, M&A dollar volume returned to the average 1986 pace. The continued strength was due in large part to another major change in the federal tax laws. This change was the lowering of the corporate tax rate, from the 1986 rate of 46 percent down to 40 percent in 1987 and 34 percent thereafter.

The change in the corporate tax rate didn't dramatically affect pricing in leveraged deals, as the debt in such transactions creates a large interest expense that wipes out much of the taxable income. The new rate did, however, make a significant difference in valuations by companies that had to pay taxes, such as non-leveraged corporate acquirers.

As a result, there was a sizeable increase in the value of businesses being sold to corporate buyers. To understand this, consider the example of an operation being divested that had annual pre-tax income of $100 million.

Under the old rate, this business would pay $46 million in federal taxes if acquired by a corporate buyer, leaving net income of $54 million. Since non-leveraged companies (usually) have to pay taxes, valuations by such purchasers are based on "price-earnings," or "PE" ratios (i.e., price divided by annual *after-tax* income), rather than cash-flow multiples. Using a PE ratio of 14 (the stock-market average in 1987), the value of the operation to the taxpaying corporate acquirer would be $54 million x 14 PE = $756 million under the 46 percent rate. But at the new tax rate of 34 percent, net income would be $66 million. Thus a 14 PE would result in a valuation of $924 million—or a 22 percent increase in value.

Hence, corporate purchasers would now pay much higher prices for acquisitions. These buyers—who were piling up cash in the economic recovery and seeking growth strategies—began to fight over operations being divested from leveraged deals. As a result, the M&A market resumed its prosperity in 1987, making it easy for acquirers to sell off pieces in "break-up" deals—and thereby further fueling leverage actions.

Selling off operations and assets was a part of leveraged deals since day one. Typically every such transaction is supposed to include the promise of a few divestitures in the first year in order to pay off a portion of the debt. This pleases the commercial-bank lenders to see some tangible results from the buyout plan. Most important, these sales cut the lenders' risk, as much of their loan is paid back right away.

In fact, many of the early leveraged deals (such as Metromedia) were fantastic successes precisely because they were complete break-ups. And in the hot M&A market of 1986–87, the Beatrice LBO also became a megahit. As was alluded to above, a number of the food conglomerate's large units (including Playtex, Tropicana, and Avis) were sold off at high prices—which returned most of the $6 billion purchase price and left what appeared to be $3 billion of remaining value.

The break-up deals were nothing more than arbitrage on a grand scale. Companies that had a segment whose potential was yet to be appreciated by investors (such as the cellular-phone franchises owned by Metromedia) or firms with numerous nonsynergistic pieces (and thus, not easily comprehended by investors) were misunderstood and undervalued by the market. So the leverage player could come in and acquire the company cheaply from the public shareholders.

It didn't matter if the cash-flow forecasts used to sell the acquisition idea to lenders were a touch optimistic. That's because there was never really any intention of running the company and paying back the debt over a period of years. The opportunistic buyers knew what the separate pieces of the target were actually worth, and they could quickly divest large chunks. As long as M&A prices were rising and publicly traded stocks were undervalued, leverage players could be certain they would be able to sell for more than they paid. The lenders went along—as they received large fees and got their loans paid back right away from the divestiture proceeds.

Furthermore, it was obvious that prices in the M&A market would continue to rise. Eased credit policies, relaxed antitrust enforcement, declining interest rates, the stimulus provided by junk bonds, the renewed interest of corporate acquirers, and the extra boost of lower tax rates all combined to create a giant, growing bubble of optimism. Given the flawless track record of past deals, it appeared there was no risk in making a leveraged acquisition. LBOs took on a "can't-miss" aura.

Indeed, not only were deals made with the assumption that operations would be sold at favorable prices right after closing, but now companies were being sold off *even before they were taken over!* An acquirer could begin negotiations with potential buyers and have the sale of key units of the target all lined up before launching a bid. M&A became a jungle!

While LBO firms and other "friendly" acquirers were prospering in 1987, several factors were having at least a slowing effect on takeover artists. One of the most important of these changes had its origins back in 1984. That was when Household International's management received an overture from one of their board members, a principal of an LBO firm, about considering a leveraged buyout.

Household's management was not receptive to the LBO idea. The company then instituted an unusual "stock rights" plan.

Under this plan, if an outside investor (a) purchased 20 percent or more of the firm's shares or (b) made a tender offer for at least 30 percent, the shareholders could use the rights to cause Household to become prohibitively expensive to the pursuer.

The director from the LBO firm fought the rights offering in court. When the plan was upheld, the first truly lethal "poison pill" was born.*

Several types of poison pills were eventually developed, but the intent was always the same. A poison pill is designed to force a potential acquirer to negotiate with the board of directors rather than make a tender offer directly to shareholders—or to at least compel some sort of reasonably fair price and terms if the pursuer tries a hostile offer.

As a result, poison pills provided a major benefit to shareholders, in that they led to the end of the dreaded two-step transaction. No longer could a pursuer make an offer for 51 percent of a target's stock at one price and different terms for the rest, for such a purchase would

---

* There had earlier been a much-heralded poison pill instituted by Lenox, Inc., but it didn't prevent that company from ultimately being acquired by Brown-Forman Distillers Corporation.

activate the poison pill. Takeover players now had to make their intentions known before reaching the poison-pill threshold, which was usually set at 15 percent or 20 percent stock ownership. This was a major step forward in fairness, especially for small shareholders who couldn't tender as fast as big institutions. And though poison pills weren't the ultimate answer for defense, they were a significant first step. By 1987 most large, publicly traded companies had adopted one.

Important events were also occurring in commercial-bank lending for leveraged deals. As noted earlier, Citicorp, Manufacturers Hanover, and Bankers Trust achieved domination early on in senior loans for LBOs and takeovers, and became the "Big Three" of leveraged-deal bank lending. However, the huge size of deals created a need to spread lending risk. Given that other commercial banks were eager to get in on this lending, by 1987 the use of "bank syndicates" in leveraged deals was firmly established.

As mentioned earlier, the use of a syndicate is a tradition in stock and bond financings. A lead firm will originate an offering and distribute a portion of the securities itself, dividing the rest among a number of other firms. The obvious function is to disperse risk. However, syndication also helps keep the competition from getting overly aggressive, as everyone receives a slice of the pie.

Bank-loan syndication in leveraged deals worked in a similar way. A "lead" bank (or banks), almost always one or more of the Big Three, would commit to the bank-financing portion of the deal. The lead institution would keep a piece of the loan (and a large portion of the fees), then would syndicate to a number of other banks.

Furthermore, by 1987 it had become common for commercial banks to sell off leveraged-deal loans to non-bank institutions. The loan buyers were pension funds, insurance companies, mutual funds, and even savings-and-loans.[*]

---

[*] This comparison between leveraged-deal banking syndicates and investment-banking syndicates is for analysis purposes only. It is in no way intended to imply or infer that Citicorp, Manufacturers Hanover, Bankers Trust, or any other commercial bank engaged in underwriting practices regarding corporate securities.

The fees from leveraged-deal bank lending could be enormous. Besides an immediate proposal fee, there were commitment fees, origination fees, facility fees, closing fees, syndication fees, management fees, expense fees, etc. In total, the fees could add up to five percent or more of the bank loans (i.e., even greater than the mezzanine-financing fees). And bank debt was typically at least 60 percent of the funding in large leveraged deals.*

Since a key factor for success in leveraged deals was speed of financing, banks had to be willing to make lending commitments incredibly quickly, often in less than 48 hours. An obvious result of such practices was a deterioration in "due diligence" (i.e., pre-deal analysis) work. The actual market value of assets and the assumptions underlying cash-flow forecasts could easily be brushed over, as banks often had to promise funds before they had done a significant review. But such aspects didn't seem that important for these loans, as most of the loan would be syndicated, sold, or quickly repaid with divestiture proceeds. And lenders were further comforted in that not a single large company that had done a leveraged deal had yet gone under.

Prior to 1987, Drexel-financed takeover players and LBO firms had things pretty much to themselves, being able to do big leveraged deals without the fear of competition. But the swollen fees and immense returns soon attracted other participants. By 1987, all of the major investment-banking firms had LBO groups and at least rudimentary machinery to arrange leveraged-deal financings. For example, Merrill Lynch led a $4.2 billion LBO of Borg-Warner, a $1.7 billion one of Supermarkets General, and a $1.1 billion one of Fruehauf. Morgan Stanley organized the $2.2 billion buyout of Burlington Industries.

Several of the large investment bankers now took sizeable equity interests in leveraged deals, portraying themselves as "merchant bankers" in the European tradition of financial firms and lenders investing in industrial clients. (This is also a tradition in Japan, but for

---

* Recall that in 1983 a one percent bank fee was considered large.

some reason no one on Wall Street ever made that analogy.) Of course, what finally allowed the investment bankers to play and win in the LBO game was their ability to solve the speed-of-mezzanine-financing problem through the advent of bridge loans.

As you'll recall, bridge financing is a temporary loan provided by the investment-banking firm out of its own funds. In 1980s leveraged deals, such debt was used for the last portion of funding, allowing the acquirer to get the transaction done before being beaten out by competing offers. After the deal closed, the investment banker would refinance the bridge loan, usually in the public debt markets.

The event that proved bridge debt's viability was First Boston's use of this tactic in Campeau Corporation's purchase of Allied Stores. The $3.5 billion deal had to be done quickly in order to beat the tax-law changes that would go into effect at the start of 1987. First Boston wanted the deal so badly that the firm reportedly was willing to supply $1.8 billion. However, after Citibank came forward with senior debt, the bridge loan ended up being $865 million. Most important, First Boston was able to quickly replace the loan with a public offering for the client. When several of the Allied store chains were soon divested, the deal was proclaimed a winner.

Bridge debt changed the leverage game. Now any big investment-banking firm could do quick mezzanine funding; all it took was size and the ability to refinance the bridge. If other firms wanted to keep up with First Boston, they too would have to be willing to make such loans. And soon many were. In early 1987, Merrill Lynch committed to a $650 million bridge loan to wrap up the Borg-Warner LBO, and Morgan Stanley did a $600 million one to secure the buyout of glassmaker Owens-Illinois for KKR.

Leveraged deals with bridge debt were incredibly profitable for the investment banker. Instead of just a one percent M&A fee, the bridge-loaning firm received much more. There was a fee for organizing the deal, a fee for the bridge loan, and a fee for refinancing the bridge loan (i.e., the "double fee" effect). In total, the percentage fees going to the investment banker in a transaction that included bridge debt could surpass those of Drexel in its junk-financed deals.

The popularity of the bridge-loan tactic was aided by the ongoing woes of Drexel. By early 1987 the SEC's protracted investigation of Milken and Drexel was under way.

Although bridge financing lessened the influence of Drexel, the firm still ruled the junk-debt market. However, other investment bankers were now able to place large junk offerings, primarily because Milken had made such debt seem so acceptable. Many mainstream institutions were now more than willing to buy these securities.

As the institutional players became more important in the market, Milken's influence diminished. The market simply became too big for one man to dominate. Other investment-banking firms could place junk debt with institutional clients, then maintain a market in such issues. When this ability was combined with the bridge-loan tactic, these firms became true leveraged-deal players. In fact, the 1980s can be divided into two distinct epochs. First there was the era prior to the Boesky revelations, when Drexel and its takeover clients dominated via Milken's system. Then there was "after Boesky," when First Boston, Shearson Lehman, Merrill Lynch, and Morgan Stanley dominated, financing deals via their own bridge-loan and junk-financing abilities.

Although the leverage game became much more competitive after the appearance of bridge debt, in retrospect one realizes that the pre-1987 era was incredibly easy. As the economy slowly recovered from the 1982 recession, stocks were way underpriced relative to the leveraged and break-up values of companies. Not until several large deals had been successful did a belief take hold that LBOs were for real. Only then did the market begin to incorporate leverage potential into the stock prices of companies.

Also not to be forgotten were numerous tax and legal aspects that made pre-1987 leveraged deals so profitable. Prior to the 1986 tax-law changes, buyers could write up the value of acquired assets, then depreciate the assets on the higher basis. This acquisition-depreciation tax shield—in combination with the interest deduction on the debt used to finance deals—meant that leveraged-deal acquirers paid very little in taxes.

Furthermore, in break-up deals, acquirers could also use a technique known as a "mirror" transaction. The result was to defer the tax gain that came about from the divestiture of subsidiaries with low tax-basis book values. Acquirers could also take advantage of a company's overfunded pension plan, "recapturing" such assets and using the proceeds as a type of built-in financing.

By the middle of 1987, however, the salad days of leveraged deals were already coming to an end. Tax-law changes had made asset write-ups impractical and would soon end mirror transactions. Most companies with overfunded pension plans had by now done recaptures of their own.

With so many new players in the game, many proposed deals attracted rival bidders. As is the case with all arbitrage opportunities, information eventually flowed out, new people learned the game, and the opportunities were competed away. Prices of targets were bid up and returns started to drift down, especially in the highly visible multi-billion-dollar transactions. Deals were now being done at 9-, 10-, and even 12-times cash flow.

Some of the pioneers of LBOs could see that the glory days were gone and pulled back. William Simon cancelled out of a buyout fund to be raised in 1986. Jerome Kohlberg, the first name in Kohlberg Kravis Roberts, left that firm to specialize in deals "where reason prevails."

It wasn't long until some deals turned bad. Stock prices continued to go up and the economy kept expanding in 1987, but some leveraged transactions were just too stretched. The first large LBO bankruptcy was Revco Drug Stores, which filed for Chapter 11 protection in July 1988.

Although Revco wasn't a Drexel-financed LBO, it wasn't as though Drexel hadn't raised financing for any weak or faltering deals. It was simply that Milken was an expert at patching up such issues.

92 THE ANSWER

When a Drexel-distributed junk issue got in trouble, Milken would often rescue it by having bondholders take an "exchange offer" of a new security with more favorable terms for the issuer. The junk-debt-using/holding participants in Milken's system accepted this revised security (that is, if they wanted to avoid having a defaulted holding). And in some cases Drexel itself would buy and hold depressed bonds. It was clearly in Milken's interest to perform this function of rescuing such issues, in order that the impression of a low default rate and safe market in junk debt be maintained. But other investment bankers, who weren't so dependent on junk securities, didn't necessarily possess the same desire to restructure financings that had problems.

Goldman suffered through a disappointing year in 1987 in terms of recap deal flow. Worse yet, First Boston was now in the recap game, advising on the $2.4 billion Holiday (Inn) Corporation deal with the assistance of Drexel.

What's more, First Boston did the landmark recap of the year, a $3 billion one for publisher Harcourt Brace Jovanovich. In this transaction, First Boston provided a billion-dollar bridge loan, which was refinanced in less than two months with a public junk-debt offering.

As leveraged-deal business was slipping away from Goldman, bridge financing became more and more tempting. There was, of course, risk in this tactic; a bridge loan held great peril if it couldn't quickly be refinanced. Nevertheless, the tactic seemed to be working for other firms. Even investment bankers without strong junk-distribution networks were easily refinancing these loans.

In 1987, Goldman, along with Salomon Brothers, provided a $600 million bridge loan for the Southland Corporation (7-Eleven stores) leveraged buyout.

Code-named "Project Heaven," the Southland deal became Project Hell for Goldman Sachs. As the bridge-loan refinancing effort got going, the 1987 stock-market crash occurred. Investors immediately became nervous about leveraged deals. Goldman and Salomon tried to sell junk bonds to replace the loan; however, institutions were reluctant to purchase Southland subordinated debt. The offering had to be revised, with equity warrants being added to one of the issues (a la Drexel), some of the bonds having interest rates of 18 percent.

Although Goldman eventually came out of the Southland deal without damage, the affair was enough to convince the firm's leaders that risking their own money in such financings wasn't necessarily a wise move. As Goldman chairman John Weinberg would observe, "We watch our eggs very carefully, because they are everything we have." One would have to be exceedingly careful before wagering equity capital built over 118 years on leveraged-deal bridge loans.

8. Barney Kroger's Grocery Wagon

The M&A bubble burst, for five months anyway, with the October 1987 stock-market crash. But once the dust had settled and it became apparent the machinery of leveraged deals was still in place, activity got going again.

By the middle of 1988, the era of the megadeal had arrived. This was the beginning of the post-crash phase of 1980s leveraged deal-making, where huge, high-priced transactions driven by bridge loans and the quest for ever-higher fees took precedence.

The list of deals in 1988 was staggering. Philip Morris bought Kraft Inc. for $13 billion. Campeau Corporation purchased Federated Department Stores for $6.5 billion. The British got in the act, with Grand Metropolitan paying $5.7 billion for Pillsbury and B.A.T. Industries acquiring Farmers Group for $5.2 billion. A $3.8 billion LBO was done at Montgomery Ward and a $3.6 billion one was done at Fort Howard Corporation. And the $25 billion RJR Nabisco LBO was still to be completed.

Goldman's most visible role in the ultra megadeals came in the Kraft versus Philip Morris affair. In October 1988, Philip Morris Companies made a $90-per-share, $11.5 billion bid for Kraft.

Kraft's stock was trading around $60 at the time; thus the $90-per-share offer was a lavish 50-percent premium. Philip Morris had, in other words, made what appeared to be a preemptive bid. It was doubtful that anyone could find financing to top the offer, especially since the attention of Shearson Lehman, KKR, Salomon, Drexel, the Big Three bank lenders and others was being focused on RJR Nabisco.

No one else jumped in to make a bid for Kraft. With Beatrice broken up, RJR Nabisco being fought over, and Pillsbury in a battle with Grand Metropolitan, there were few large food companies available to come in as a white knight. That left a recap as an alternative. Soon after the Philip Morris offer, Kraft announced an enormous plan.

The recap included $84-per-share in cash plus $14-per-share of securities. In this case, a price was immediately estimated for the stub, given as $12. That put the recap package at $110 per share, or a full *$20 per share higher* than the Philip Morris bid. Counting the stub, the total value of the Kraft plan would be $14 billion, which would make this the largest transaction to date, surpassing even the $13.2 billion Gulf/Chevron merger.

The Kraft recap appeared a bit auspicious. It was planned that $6.8 billion of bank loans would be arranged and $3 billion of subordinated debt would be placed. However, given that there was only so much leveraged-deal financing capacity in the world (and the Kraft recap would be competing for funds with a $20 billion-plus RJR Nabisco LBO), such financing would have been challenging, to say the least.

With the recap price stretched to the limit, there was little sense in any further jousting between the contestants. A meeting between the two sides ended the short saga: Kraft was acquired by Philip Morris for $106 per share. For its work, Goldman reportedly received a $30 million fee.[*]

---

[*] Possessing large holdings of stock and stock options, Kraft's management came out well as a result of the company being acquired.

Although there was a great fee for the Kraft deal, it would be even better if a large recap were actually completed, a deal that would demonstrate all the positive aspects of this tactic and prove Goldman's ability to quickly raise a large amount of subordinated financing. Such a success would establish the recap as a solid megadeal tactic. In the late summer of 1988, an opportunity arose.

The Kroger Company, a Cincinnati-based supermarket chain, was a conservative firm whose stock had been a lackluster performer during the post-crash recovery of the stock market. With its steady, recession-proof cash flows, grocery retailing was a fertile area for leverage: KKR did an LBO of Safeway Stores in 1986 and the Stop & Shop chain earlier in 1988, and Merrill Lynch had arranged an LBO of Supermarkets General in 1987. Kroger appeared to be just as good a candidate. The firm's shares had been trading in the low-to-mid-$30s throughout 1988, which translated to about four-times cash flow. Kroger also possessed valuable real-estate assets, pension plans that were significantly overfunded, and numerous ancillary operations that could be divested.

In the Safeway, Stop & Shop, and Supermarkets General affairs, Herbert Haft's Dart Group Corporation had made offers for the companies prior to the acquisitions arranged by KKR and Merrill Lynch. In fact, in five cases since 1985, Dart Group had made offers or bought stakes in companies prior to large LBOs being done by other firms, such cases including another KKR deal, the Beatrice LBO. Consequently, if there were someone for Kroger to be on the lookout for, it was Dart Group.

In August 1988, there was a period of unusual trading activity in Kroger shares. During that month, a Haft entity had made a Hart-Scott-Rodino ("HSR") filing for antitrust clearance regarding Kroger, but didn't make a public announcement of the filing (such an announcement is optional). Kroger's management knew of the HSR filing, as the target company is informed of such requests.

On September 9, the Federal Trade Commission notified Herbert Haft that he had approval to purchase additional shares of Kroger. If he remained true to form, an offer for Kroger could be expected at any time.

On September 13, Kroger and Goldman got off the first shot. The supermarket firm announced plans for a $4 billion-plus recap.

The Kroger recap would include a $40-per-share cash distribution and $8-per-share worth of discount debentures. No official price estimate was given for the stub shares. Analysts estimated the stub value at about $6, and the total package at roughly $54 per share.

Haft still didn't do anything. Then again, maybe he didn't have to, since Kroger had taken action by announcing a recap. But in order for KKR to be able to approach a management in a rescue mode, there had to be an announced threat of some sort. On September 19, a proposal of cash and securities valued at $55 per share came from Dart Group.

The question now was how long before KKR would arrive on the scene. Yet by acting first, Kroger had effectively destroyed any justification for KKR making an approach. Why would Kroger now need a rescue when it already had its own defense/wealth-creation plan put together?

For KKR to do an LBO here, a novel basis to approach Kroger would be needed. And in order for a proposal to be successful, it would have to be clearly superior to the recap plan.

Soon after Dart Group's bid, KKR played its hand by making a proposal—but with an interesting twist. The LBO firm proposed to acquire Kroger for $50-per-share in cash plus $6.50-per-share in debt securities. However, KKR also included in the package *a partial stub share of the post-buyout Kroger*, which was estimated to be worth $2. The total value of the package was $58.50 per share.

With KKR having to make an "uninvited" proposal, this was a somewhat embarrassing day for the LBO firm. Since Kroger had achieved a head start in preparing and announcing the recap plan, KKR was forced to react to the supermarket firm's moves.

Kroger fired right back. On September 23, the Kroger board rejected the KKR and Dart Group proposals and approved the recap plan. The company said that commitments had been offered for more than $3 billion of bank financing. Kroger also stated that Goldman was "highly confident" of being able to arrange the required subordinated debt.

But Kroger and Goldman had now played *their* hand by estimating a value for the stub share in Kroger's recap. This was given as a range of $9 to $13—thereby producing a total immediate value of between $57 and $61 per share for the recap package.

Goldman did not do a huge amount of business with KKR during this period. Hence, there didn't seem to be any reason why either side would pull any punches in the affair. And if the recap tactic could meet a firm like KKR head-on and win, it would be a huge boost for Goldman's status as a leveraged-deal advisor.

On October 4, a letter from KKR arrived at Kroger. The buyout firm now proposed a $64-per-share deal. The plan consisted of still $50-per-share in cash, but with $11-per-share of debt securities and a $3 stub.

The KKR plan had a further key provision. It was stated that if Kroger went ahead and paid the recap distribution, KKR proposed to acquire the Kroger stub shares *after the recap* for the price of $10 cash and a $3.50 debenture. Under this scenario, the total value to the stockholder would be $61.50 per share (i.e., the $48 Kroger cash-and-debt distribution plus $13.50 from KKR). It therefore behooved Kroger's management and board to deeply consider the KKR $64-per-share proposal—lest they risk incurring the wrath of their stockholders for allowing a lesser result.

The KKR letter presented a problem for the recap. In approving the recap, the Kroger board had concluded that the plan "would provide greater value to the company's shareholders" than either the Dart Group's or KKR's (original) proposal.

However, KKR had now ostensibly defeated that point. The buyout firm's $64-per-share proposal provided more immediate estimated value than the Kroger plan (and $10 more cash-per-share in any case), and it also allowed outside stockholders to retain an equity interest. If Kroger wished to reject the LBO firm's overtures, some fresh reasoning would be desirable.

One might ask why the value of the recap plan couldn't be raised above KKR's proposal, perhaps by increasing the value of the discount debentures? The answer was that such a move might not be wise in this case, for two reasons.

Number one, since KKR's proposal(s) had $10 more cash-per-share than Kroger's recap, it would be best if any increase in the grocery-firm's plan were in the form of additional cash in the distribution. But promising more cash would be risky. Given that the bank lenders had already committed to finance almost 70 percent of the recap, any additional cash would likely have to come from placing more subordinated debt. Yet it was planned that the Kroger recap would require $1 billion of subordinated financing as it was. While Goldman had improved mezzanine-financing abilities, it wouldn't be wise to risk overextending such abilities.

More important, a key tenet of the recap plan was that the company was *not for sale*. Kroger was simply doing a restructuring and paying a big dividend. And since the Kroger plan had been announced before any outside offer was made, it was not a counter to an existing bid. These elements were important if Kroger intended to reject KKR's proposal. But if the recap plan were increased even one nickel, it would present the appearance of a bidding contest—and thereby might encourage pursuers to argue that Kroger should entertain outside offers.

On October 7, Kroger's board held a meeting. At such meeting, the board concluded that KKR's proposals were "subject to numerous uncertainties... includ[ing]... receipt of necessary financing." (This was even though KKR had ready access to billions of dollars of funding.)

Goldman gave an opinion that KKR's proposals were "inadequate." Yet if the LBO firm's proposals were inadequate, then the Kroger plan had to be inadequate also, right?

Actually, no. Since the Kroger plan was not a sale of the company, it did not have to be judged against the standard of a selling price.

The Kroger plan was structured as a dividend distribution, and as such, it didn't require a shareholder vote. Kroger's directors had the final say in this matter; the $4 billion-plus recap could be enacted on their approval. Even though both of KKR's existing proposals ostensibly provided more immediate value than the $61-per-share valuation of the Kroger plan, the grocery-chain's board rejected KKR's proposals and proceeded with the recap. Period. Case closed. Done deal.[*]

KKR's first response was that it was "outraged." Then the LBO firm seemed to give in. On October 11, KKR withdrew its proposals and said it didn't anticipate making any more. The recap had won.

The next task was to get the financing wrapped up quickly. And it was. One billion dollars in subordinated funding was issued in three-weeks' time from the date the KKR proposals were rejected. The debt was then refinanced three months later in the public markets.

Better yet, there were huge rewards. There was almost $60 million in total subordinated-debt financing fees, plus Goldman's advisory fee for the recap of $25 million.

The Kroger deal demonstrated important aspects of the recap tactic. It showed that such a plan could be accomplished with only board-of-directors' approval. It showed that the "not a sale of the company" aspect could help allow the target to spurn outside proposals. The result was that the recap tactic could be the consummate preemptor of

---

[*] It should be noted that KKR's (and Dart Group's) overtures for Kroger were simply proposals addressed to the company, not tender offers to the shareholders. In the case of a hostile tender offer (as at Warnaco), the decision of whether to pursue the recap was ultimately in the hands of shareholders as they decided whether to tender their shares.

any pursuer, even one as rich and powerful as KKR. Although the Kroger affair received little publicity, its importance in the history of the 1980s should not be underestimated. This deal had established that with proper preparation and adequate financing ability, the recap could outdo a seemingly invincible competitor.

Nineteen eighty-eight was a good year for Goldman in terms of leveraged-deal activity. Besides Kroger, the firm advised on large recaps at USG Corporation and Santa Fe Southern Pacific Corporation, and performed a key takeover defense for American Standard.

Kroger, however, was the success that made the year for Goldman and reestablished the firm's leveraged-deal status. The momentum and confidence provided by this recap was crucial, especially considering Goldman's virtual non-role in the most lucrative deal of 1988, the RJR Nabisco LBO saga.

Goldman, like every major investment-banking firm, tried to find a way into the RJR Nabisco party. When this battle became a sort-of auction, Goldman teamed with the LBO firm Forstmann Little to organize a bidding group for the food/tobacco giant. The team included Goldman clients Procter & Gamble, Ralston Purina, and Castle & Cooke.

The late-arriving group soon bowed out of the RJR Nabisco bidding. It would have been difficult to compete in this deal anyway. The Big Three bank lenders were already in league with the top-competing Shearson Lehman and KKR teams. And an RJR Nabisco transaction couldn't be done without massive junk financing. The biggest deal of all time would require the majesty of Drexel to fill in the huge mezzanine layer.

However, being in a team with three large food/consumer-products companies didn't hurt Goldman's chances of securing a divestiture assignment from the eventual acquirer of RJR Nabisco. It would be prudent for the victor to throw a little of the work to a firm that had close relationships with rich potential buyers. Unfortunately for Goldman, the RJR Nabisco winner turned out to be KKR, the firm that had been "outraged" in the Kroger affair. There was no way that Goldman would get work on the LBO firm's most important deal ever, right?

KKR had always spread around the work in its deals, using numerous investment bankers for advice and to assist with financing and divestitures. And as it turned out, KKR didn't hold anything against its Kroger-deal opponent. The LBO firm provided Goldman the job of divesting the huge Del Monte units.

While Goldman was all ready to do more recaps, a strange thing happened. The leverage game began to slow down.

Part of the reason for the decrease in activity were the legal problems at Drexel. After a two-year investigation, the SEC filed suit against the firm in September 1988. Drexel eventually made an agreement with the U.S. Attorney to plead guilty to six felony counts and pay $650 million in fines and penalties. With the investigation focused on Milken, the junk-bond leader was indicted on criminal charges in March 1989 and departed from the firm.

An indication of increased caution by junk buyers came from the Campeau/Federated deal. First Boston tried to do an offering of $1.15 billion of Federated junk bonds to refinance its portion of a huge bridge loan, but could sell only about $750 million, even at interest rates as high as 17.75 percent.

Goldman experienced a slow year in 1989 in terms of large recap work. In M&A, an industry ranking put the firm fourth for the year in dollar volume of transactions, behind Morgan Stanley, First Boston, and the new firm of Wasserstein Perella.

However, these were the waning months of the Roaring Eighties. On October 13, 1989, the leverage era officially came to an end.

9. Crash and Burn

On September 1, 1989, a leveraged-buyout proposal was made for UAL Corporation, the parent of United Air Lines, by an investor group consisting of the Air Line Pilots Association, British Airways, and UAL's senior management. The price was an astounding $300 per share (for a company that had been trading below $120 three months earlier).

The LBO proposal had some unusual features. For one thing, the more than $7 billion of financing required for the deal would consist almost entirely of bank loans. There would be very little of the typical mezzanine funding, and no junk bonds at all.

Then there were the forecasts that underpinned the bid. These were, one might say, somewhat on the optimistic side. Although UAL had experienced an upswing in results over the past two and a half years, this company was extremely cyclical. From 1979 through 1988, UAL had *cumulative* operating profits of only $970 million, and $665 million of that came in 1988. The exact results were as follows:

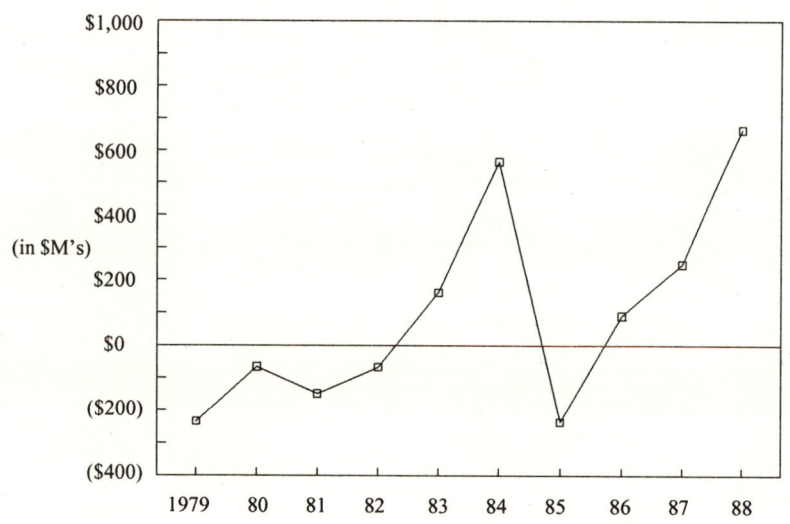

Source: UAL Corporation Annual Report for 1989, pages 10–11

Given the trend shown above, what would be a basis on which to project future results? The UAL buyout group simply assumed continuing growth from 1988 forward. Shown on the following page is the buyout group's projection for operating profit:

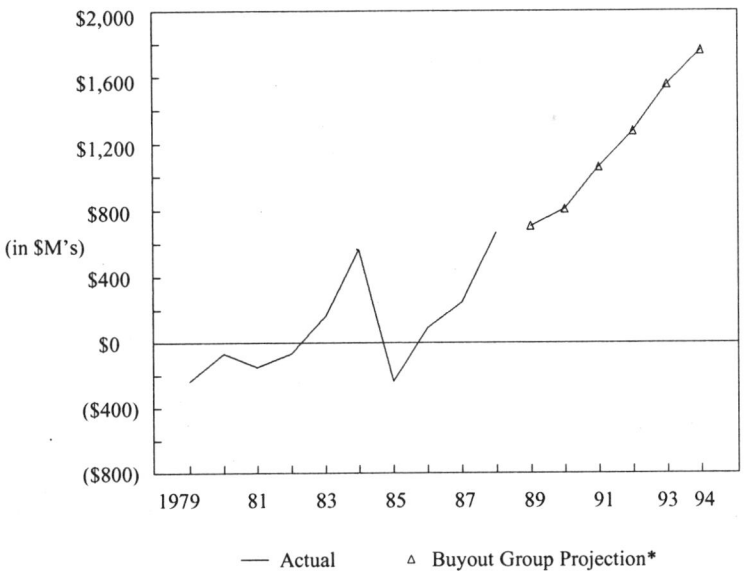

UAL Corporation Operating Profit
1979-1988 History and 1989-1994 Projection of Buyout Group

— Actual   △ Buyout Group Projection*

Source: Airline Acquisition Corp. Schedules 14D-1 dated 9/25/89 and 10/2/89

* Excludes Assumed ESOP Financing Expense

The projections had double-digit percentage growth in revenues, profits, and cash flow for each of the next five years. Although United's load factor (i.e., percentage of seats filled) had never been higher than 67.9 percent (and had been as low as 58.4 percent) during the 1979 through 1988 period, the projections were based on maintaining a 67 percent load factor.

Citicorp was to lead the bank financing in the deal. The bank committed to lend $2 billion. Chase Manhattan chipped in with a $1 billion lending commitment. Citicorp and Chase then went about arranging an additional $4 billion. However, the auspicious forecasts caused concern among potential lenders.

So the UAL deal was where it finally happened: other banks said no. After reviewing the buyout proposal, a group of commercial banks rejected participation in the financing.

As anyone involved with leveraged deals will remember, the day of the banks' rejection of the UAL deal—Friday the 13th of October 1989—was the day that the decade of debt came to an end. For the failure of this financing started a chain of events that brought the leverage world crashing down.

In the autumn of 1989, the junk-bond market was entering a state of turmoil (discussed below). This resulted in a paucity of takeover action. The proposed UAL buyout and an affair at American Airlines (whose parent company AMR Corporation had recently received a $120-per-share bid from Donald Trump) were the main contests going on at the time, and the arbitragers were heavily into these stocks.

However, the banks' reluctance to fund the United Air Lines LBO was the signal that the leverage market had been anticipating. Commercial banks had always been incredibly eager to finance leveraged deals. Their sudden hesitation in the UAL buyout—combined with a lack of junk financing (and therefore, a scarcity of bridge loans)—meant there no longer was any takeover financing that could be counted on. And without takeover financing, there no longer were any takeover candidates.

News of the banks' rejection started a flurry in the trading of stocks (formerly) considered to be takeover candidates. Trading in UAL's shares had been halted even before the news of the banks' rejection reached investors. Arbs thus tried to sell their AMR Corporation (American Airlines) holdings. But the selling pressure in AMR's shares caused trading in that stock to also be suspended. So the arbs tried to sell other stocks. This created a downward spiral in the prices of those issues, which—due to computerized trading—soon carried into the entire market.

The Dow Jones Industrial Average fell by 154 points in just over an hour on Friday the 13th; it was down 190 points (a seven percent decline) for the day. This was the second-largest point drop ever to that time, surpassed only by "Black Monday" of the 1987 crash.

Trading in UAL's shares resumed on Monday. The stock finished that session at $222.875, off a whopping $56.875 from Friday's last price. AMR Corporation, which had traded above $107 a week and a half earlier, closed at $76.50 on Monday. But as it became evident that the financing difficulties affected mainly leveraged companies and leveraged deals, the rest of the market recovered. The Dow Jones Industrials rose 88 points on Monday. In a few weeks the average had come back to its pre-UAL-rejection level.

UAL continued to slide. The stock closed at $198 on Tuesday. By the end of the week, the shares had fallen to $168.50, a 40 percent drop in just six trading days. Citing a "recent change in market conditions," Donald Trump called off his bid for AMR Corporation, which soon traded below $70. The arbs were now sitting with an estimated $600 million of paper losses on their UAL holdings.

The banks' action had done more than send a message to the UAL buyout group. The events of the ensuing week proved it was over for the leverage game; the music had finally stopped. The most conclusive evidence came from the state of the junk market.

The junk market first exhibited serious problems earlier in 1989, as a number of issues went into default. But this wasn't an overnight dilemma. The factors behind these troubles had been building for the past five years.

As was mentioned earlier, the first visible blows to the junk market were Drexel's guilty plea to six felony counts in late 1988 and Milken's indictment and forced separation from the firm soon thereafter. Yet Milken had shown it was possible to rescue troubled issues and keep the market together. From 1983 through 1988, Drexel-placed junk had a surprisingly low default rate of less than three percent. So why couldn't Drexel keep the market going? Why all the trouble now with defaults? How could these problems have been avoided for so long?

The reasons for the long halcyon period in this market were several. First, many of the early junk issues were from good deals. Furthermore, the economy had expanded almost continuously from 1983 through 1988, which allowed most leveraged firms to earn enough cash flow to meet interest payments. And when such companies did have problems, there was the opportunity to sell off assets in the M&A market.

However, the biggest factor hiding the inherent problems of junk was the action of Drexel itself in saving faltering issues. As mentioned, this was done by virtue of exchange offers, refinancing, and if necessary buying up the troubled debt.

So why couldn't Drexel keep performing these market-saving tactics?

Drexel wasn't getting sufficient revenue from new junk offerings, for a number of reasons. Of course, the firm was hurt by the government investigation and a $650 million penalty. Drexel also missed the talent and tactics of Milken himself. But the firm's main problem was that others had now taken much of its business, precisely because (as explained earlier) Milken did such a good job of sustaining the market and making junk look respectable. For the past two years, other investment-banking firms had been able to capture major deals by employing bridge loans, then selling junk debt to their institutional clients.

While Drexel was leading the financing for fewer major deals and reaping less in fees, the firm was soon to be overwhelmed by the volume of distressed issues. In order to keep the junk market going and prices stable, Drexel had to hold large amounts of troubled bonds. But without large revenue coming in, it became difficult to continue this activity. And in order to stay competitive in the leverage game, the firm had been arranging financing for risky, marginal deals—which only made the default problems worse.

In the spring of 1989, signs of Drexel's weakness began to appear. For William Farley's purchase of West Point-Pepperell, Drexel had issued a highly confident letter saying it could refinance a $1.1 billion bank-supplied bridge loan—then failed to deliver.

But the big signal came in June. One of Drexel's best clients, Integrated Resources, couldn't refinance its commercial paper. In such a situation, Drexel would normally rescue the client, often by purchasing the paper for its own account. However, in this case it didn't happen, and Integrated Resources defaulted on its debt. The lack of a rescue of such a key player was a clear indication that Drexel's days—and the junk market's—were numbered.

After the Integrated Resources default, uncertainty about junk was exacerbated when the trading in such securities more or less shut down on several occasions. To understand how this could happen in a $200 billion market, one must appreciate a few aspects of the junk-securities market itself.

During this period, junk debt was traded almost entirely through an "over-the-counter" market (rather than through an organized exchange in the manner of the highly regulated markets for stocks). There wasn't the same free flow of information as with other securities. Buyers and sellers of junk were not so easily matched.*

In the 1980s, Drexel would make a market in junk securities. Eventually other investment bankers underwrote a significant amount of these securities and made markets.

Yet these other firms did not have the incentive to maintain the same degree of liquidity in junk as Drexel did. For Drexel, junk securities had become the basis of the firm's livelihood. The competing investment bankers, on the other hand, had numerous thriving businesses. Junk was just a sideline to them.

Hence, absent Drexel's stabilizing efforts, when those firms that dealt in junk didn't feel like trading, there was no market. And as the economy slowed and a growing number of junk-financed companies faced default, everyone was trying to sell.

Yet buyers wouldn't appear and the trading wouldn't start until prices became attractive. Because junk is the lowest form of debt, it often behaves more like equity than debt. It is such a marginal security

---

* Some junk bonds were traded on traditional bond exchanges, but generally without the volume or liquidity of investment-grade issues.

that when concern over the potential default of an issue starts, the price can slide dramatically before anyone is willing to buy. Without Drexel's market-supporting tactics, the supply and demand curves now intersected at the real price—which was often a rather depressed level. It became apparent that junk bonds were actually risky and volatile securities, just as had been thought prior to Milken's arrival. They were not at all the stable and respectable instrument they had been made to appear.

Once prices began to head down, the situation snowballed. The specter of junk defaults caused institutions to want to divest such holdings. Investors withdrew funds from the numerous junk-bond mutual funds that now existed, creating further selling pressure. The junk market had survived problems such as the Boesky affair, the Revco bankruptcy, and Black Monday, but now the time had come to pay the bills—and there wasn't the cash flow, the divestiture market, or the Milken magic to postpone the inevitable. Campeau Corporation provided the ultimate blow.

Campeau Corporation was unable to come close to making its required cash flow for the Federated Department Stores acquisition. In September 1989, the company put the Bloomingdale's store chain up for sale, but was unable to find a buyer at an attractive price. Campeau had to be rescued from its cash crunch by an emergency loan from a large real-estate firm—thereby creating even more concern in the market. Like huge, toppling dominos, Campeau's problems helped push the junk market over the edge while UAL was the last straw for leveraged-deal bank lenders.

In the wake of Campeau Corporation's problems, junk prices took a beating. By the time of the banks' rejection of the UAL deal, some issues were being quoted at less than 70 percent of face value. But this was nothing compared to what was to come.

The market continued to cave in. In November 1989, Drexel laid off employees in its junk-bond department for the first time. The default rate for junk debt had exceeded five percent (of total publicly traded junk outstanding) in 1989; it would come close to 10 percent in 1990.

Other factors arose to wipe out any remaining leveraged-deal lending. Problems with savings-and-loans had put the federal government on notice to avert a similar disaster in the commercial-banking system. Regulators thus began reviewing "highly leveraged transaction" (HLT) loan portfolios of the major banks. Some banks had huge HLT exposure, the top ten holders of such loans possessing more than $45 billion in total.*

The reaction of many banks was to cut back on new lending. This worsened the 1990 credit crunch and intensified the recessionary environment. The result was that it was all the harder for leveraged companies to achieve their promised cash flows.

With a lack of bank and junk financing, the already depressed M&A market took a nosedive. LBO activity, especially by the smaller acquirers that were dependent on bank funding, dried up. The industrial firms that were up to their necks in junk debt from 1980s leveragings had to make divestitures, and thus there were a large number of businesses for sale. However, as Campeau's experience showed, the buyers weren't there, even for well-known operations the likes of Bloomingdale's. M&A prices and activity sank. Total dollar volume in the second quarter of 1990 was less than half the level of the previous year, and at the lowest annual pace since 1983.

By early 1990, public junk financings had all but disappeared. Volume for 1990 was a mere *5 percent* of the previous year's amount. After creating more than $900 million in disclosed fees in 1988, the underwriting of junk bonds produced a total of *less than $20 million in fees* for all of 1990. The junk market was back to what it had been before Milken, a small and risky netherworld of corporate finance.

Drexel received more than $200 million for its RJR Nabisco work, which helped save the company for a time. But this financing was the junk-bond firm's last hurrah.

---

* Thankfully, federal regulations prohibited commercial banks from directly owning junk bonds.

At the beginning of 1990, Drexel had a huge inventory of depressed securities. With an absence of new deals, the business was gone. The firm faced an insurmountable liquidity crunch; this time it was Drexel that couldn't refinance its commercial paper. On February 13, 1990, the firm filed for what would effectively become a terminal bankruptcy.

Part III.
REDEMPTION

10. You Can Go Home Again

As the decade of the 1990s took shape, Goldman was back on top. The firm was once again a leader in its key businesses of underwriting and M&A. While several of the other major investment-banking firms were constrained by the wreckage of their 1980s excesses, Goldman had reestablished advantages in all of the important markets and was positioned to benefit from the latest trends.

Traditional underwriting resumed en masse in 1991, for several reasons. To begin with, a decline in interest rates prompted healthy companies to refinance their old, high-cost debt with new issues. The reduced interest rates also meant that earnings and cash flows were being discounted by the market at a lower rate. Thus stock prices were pushed up. The strong stock prices—combined with the demise of junk and general aversion to debt—led to deleveraging through equity offerings. Numerous companies became convinced it was time to sell shares. The result was a deluge of financing work. Both stock and bond underwriting hit record levels in 1991, with total volume almost double the previous all-time high.

Goldman—with its many corporate and institutional contacts and extensive capital sources—possessed the elements needed to take advantage of the current opportunities. In 1991, the firm was second in total domestic underwriting volume, and number one in the lucrative equity-underwriting market.

An active area of equity underwriting in 1991 were "reverse LBOs." These were the cash-out offerings of firms that had undergone buyouts, where the investors were now selling some or all of the equity (often using a portion of the proceeds to reduce debt, and thus creating the reverse effect of the original leveraging).

The reverse LBOs included large issues from KKR's holdings. And Goldman was there as an underwriter, playing a major role in the equity offerings of Stop & Shop, Safeway, and Duracell. Goldman's expertise was employed in the LBO firm's most important financings, including the lead in a $1.3 billion issue of RJR Nabisco common stock.

Goldman was in command in other underwriting markets. The firm's bond operations had recovered from their 1980s problems. What's more, Goldman had become a top underwriter of junk debt!

Though junk all but vanished in 1990 (only 10 public issues were done the entire year), this form of financing returned in 1991 with several large offerings, including billion-dollar issues by Owens-Illinois and RJR Nabisco. This was a different kind of junk funding, however. It was not for takeovers, but was more a means of refinancing by the large and stable leveraged firms. Goldman was ready, leading an offering for KKR's Safeway Stores.[*]

---

[*] Goldman was also in position to benefit from another opportunity arising from the demise of leverage. The firm began to invest in the securities of struggling leveraged companies, attempting to reap gains as such securities were bought out or revised when these companies undertook financial restructurings. Goldman did achieve some large gains in this practice. However, when the firm's public role in this activity—which included the purchase of securities of former leveraged-deal clients—brought a backlash from the financial and corporate communities, Goldman greatly scaled back its role.

In 1990 the M&A game was back to what it had been before Milken: investment bankers advising large corporations on strategic acquisitions. Since this practice had always been a Goldman strength, the firm returned to a solid number one position in the field. In fact, Goldman was even representing both sides of deals again, advising both Avery International Corporation and Dennison Manufacturing in their 1990 merger.

How did Goldman come out on top? The firm prevailed in the leverage era for a number of reasons, yet a key to its success was the firm's affinity with corporate managements. Goldman eventually triumphed over Drexel because Goldman was on the side of the CEO and board-of-directors power bases. Once Goldman acquired the tools to compete with the junk-financed players, its clients had all the advantage in the leverage game; for a properly armed incumbent management has a big edge in any takeover battle. Goldman capitalized on this aspect and based its 1980s actions on it. While others backed aggressors, Goldman had the foresight to aid an investment banker's long-term friends—i.e., corporate managements.

In this process, Goldman persuaded executives through a relationship of trust. The policy of not representing hostile bidders was important. While others firms would sometimes try to use fear to induce a leverage action, Goldman convinced executives they had a friend looking out for their interests. With much mistrust of investment bankers in this period, Goldman's approach was ideal. The firm was thus able to use the motives of such executives to spur them to leverage action.

There was another reason for Goldman's success, which was the attitude of the firm's people. Goldman people (in almost all cases) maintained an aura of professionalism and dignity in this difficult period for corporate America. They treated their dealings with management as a long-term relationship, thereby inspiring confidence. If a leveraging was done, it was handled with propriety and efficiency.

When advising a management, Goldman Sachs—almost uniquely among investment bankers in this period—had patience.

While Goldman prospered in the wake of the leverage era, other participants suffered from the baggage they still held. One group was the commercial-bank lenders.

Why had major commercial banks fought over leveraged-deal lending? Their behavior was due to several factors. They were drawn in by huge fees. Banks competing for leveraged-deal loans had little means to differentiate themselves other than through price and speed. Consequently, they hurried their due-diligence procedures.

The banks were comforted by the apparent success of the early leveraged deals. They thought they could cut their risk by requiring significant divestitures; all seemed fine as long as the leveraged companies completed their asset sales, paid down a big chunk of their debt, and made their interest payments. After a while, many banks didn't even bother to scrutinize the cash-flow forecasts of leveraged deals.

It was also believed that banks could truly spread their risk via syndication, taking only a small piece of each deal. But when a large portion of the market has problems, a syndicate is no protection. And there was a consistent short-term attitude that permeated the bank lending process. The competition often wasn't to get the best loans, but rather the highest up-front fees. Lending officers could maximize their personal wealth by bringing in fee-heavy loans, then get a promotion or head for another bank—leaving someone else to deal with the problems.

At the beginning of the new decade, many of Goldman's investment-banking competitors were suffering. The reason? Most of the major Wall Street firms took a short-term, live-for-today attitude regarding leveraged deals, striving for instant-fee gratification. The Drexel threat caused them to fight among themselves for business—instead of acting for their own common good as in the hierarchy days of underwriting.

Most of the other firms focused only on the upside of leverage, virtually ignoring the impact of the downfall of debt. To even the casual observer there was evidence of the inevitable demise of leverage: Besides the history of such crazes, there were advance signals early in the 1980s from the boom-to-bust markets in oil and farmland and the collapse of real-estate syndicators. Yet most of the other firms didn't properly prepare for the conclusion of the game. It was Goldman that best employed the long-term approach.

First Boston suffered greatly. While Goldman avoided risking its own capital on bridge debt, First Boston did the opposite, committing huge amounts for bridge loans in the pursuit of a merchant-banking strategy. The result was that in mid-1990, First Boston was still saddled with more than $1 billion of bridge loans, including $250 million from bankrupt Campeau/Federated.

A billion dollars of troubled bridge loans were a problem for a firm that only had equity of about $1 billion. Luckily, First Boston had its own banking connection in Crédit Suisse. In 1990, Crédit Suisse's parent provided an assistance package that consisted of a $300 million equity infusion and the backing of a partnership that bought up most of the bridge loans. But the salvation carried a major price: The Crédit Suisse holding company would now hold a majority interest in First Boston's parent firm.

Other investment bankers had leveraged-deal baggage. Shearson Lehman still held a $500 million bridge loan in mid-1992. In 1990, Kidder Peabody sold $750 million in junk bonds, bridge loans, and other leveraged-deal holdings to parent General Electric. Salomon Brothers had a lawsuit from Revco securities holders on its hands. In early 1990, Merrill Lynch took a $470 million write-off, much of it related to junk bonds, and announced it would reduce its staff by 3,000. In fact, the securities industry in total became 50,000 persons lighter between the 1987 stock-market crash and 1992. Meanwhile, a healthy Goldman began adding people in 1990.

Goldman had won the leverage war. It had won by building advantages. It had triumphed by utilizing trust, by being on the side of corporate managements, and by competing through the entire leverage cycle. It was now a huge and dominant firm. In its fiscal 1991, Goldman reportedly had pre-tax profits of $1.15 billion, and partners' capital was $3 billion at year's end. The firm had prevailed by utilizing the lessons of Sidney Weinberg to achieve Gus Levy's ideal. In the end, Goldman Sachs had succeeded in being Long-Term Greedy.

About the Author

During the 1980s, Nils Lindskoog worked as a corporate mergers-and-acquisitions professional. A graduate of Northwestern University's J.L. Kellogg Graduate School of Management, he held various financial-management and corporate-development positions with a large electronics company, a diversified industrial firm, and a unit of a financial-services company. His work included leveraged-deal and takeover-defense analysis, culminating in a major role in a leveraged recapitalization advised on by Goldman Sachs.

Acknowledgements

For their assistance, the author thanks the Elmhurst (Illinois) Public Library, the Elmhurst College Library, the Chicago Public Library, the Chicago office of the U.S. Securities and Exchange Commission, and Alexander Greenfeld.

Notes and References

This book is the result of nine years of experience and research on Goldman Sachs and the financial events of the 1980s. During the 1980s and early 1990s, I worked as a corporate mergers-and-acquisitions professional, having extensive contact with investment bankers and other financial professionals in regard to leveraged-deal proposals and analysis, sale and purchase of companies, and takeover defenses. My experience included a key role in a leveraged recapitalization by an industrial firm advised by Goldman Sachs. The information contained herein comes from such work, including my direct experiences with personnel of Goldman Sachs and other investment-banking firms and financial firms, and from research regarding the events described.

The pages stated for each article are the only pages being referenced for that respective citation.

INTRODUCTION – Notes

page 11 The pre-tax profit of Goldman Sachs & Company for its 1991 fiscal year reportedly was stated in a confidential offering circular of private-placement notes of Goldman Sachs filed in September 1992, as reported in Michael Siconolfi, "Goldman Sachs Is Earnings King on Wall Street, With Record 1991 Pretax Profit of $1.15 Billion," *Wall Street Journal*, September 22, 1992, p. C1, and in Adam Bryant, "Glimpse of Goldman Sachs: Pretax Profit of $1.15 Billion," *New York Times*, September 22, 1992, pp. D1 and D19, details of the Goldman offering circular originally being reported in Michael Liebowitz, "Goldman Raises $200 Million in Private Debt Market," *Investment Dealers' Digest*, September 21, 1992, pp. 5–6.

CHAPTER 1 – Notes

pages 15–17 The early history of Goldman Sachs and the initial offering of Sears Roebuck stock are described in Barry E. Supple, "A Business Elite: German-Jewish Financiers in Nineteenth-Century New York," *Business History Review*, Summer 1957, pp. 147, 155, 156,

170–171, and 172–174, and in Michael Jensen, *The Financiers* (New York: Weybright and Talley, 1976), pp. 191–194.

pages 18–19 The activities and structure of Goldman Sachs Trading Corporation are described in Michael Jensen, *The Financiers* (New York: Weybright and Talley, 1976), p. 197; in Benjamin J. Stein, "You Can Bank on It: Without Glass-Steagall, History Will Repeat," *Barron's*, February 4, 1991, pp. 16–17; and in John Kenneth Galbraith, *A Short History of Financial Euphoria* (Whittle Books, 1990), pp. 58–59. Goldman Sachs Trading Corporation's purchase of the stock of commercial banks and insurance companies and the use of these entities' funds to purchase securities underwritten by Goldman Sachs is described by Stein. The use of multiple mutual funds by Goldman Sachs Trading Corporation is described by Galbraith.

pages 20–21 The hierarchy of securities underwriting is described in Samuel L. Hayes III, "The Transformation of Investment Banking," *Harvard Business Review*, January-February 1979, pp. 153–155, and was originally described in Hayes' "Investment Banking: Power Structure in Flux," *Harvard Business Review*, March-April 1971.

page 21 Business practices of Sidney Weinberg are described in Garry Evans, "The Weinberg Interview," *Euromoney*, June 1990, p. 36; in Cary Reich, "Interview with John Whitehead," *Institutional Investor*, June 1987, p. 27; in Jack Willoughby, "Can Goldman Stay on Top?" *Forbes*, September 18, 1989, p. 160; in Robert J. Cole, "Low-Profile Leader Takes Charge," *New York Times*, August 16, 1984, p. D5; and in Thomas Easton, "Golden Reign Ends at Goldman Sachs," *Baltimore Sun*, August 26, 1990.

pages 22–23 The sale of Penn Central commercial paper by Goldman Sachs prior to Penn Central's bankruptcy filing and subsequent claims against Goldman Sachs are described in Michael Jensen, *The Financiers* (New York: Weybright and Talley, 1976), pp. 189–190 and 199–205. Penn Central's condition prior to its bankruptcy filing is described in "The Penn Central's Misguided Gamble," *Business Week*, June 27, 1970, pp. 96–100, and in Martin Mayer, *The Bankers* (New York: Weybright and Talley, 1974), pp. 305–308. Testimony of Gus Levy regarding the sale of Penn Central commercial paper by Goldman Sachs is discussed by Jensen. The SEC investigation and findings regarding the sale of Penn Central commercial paper by Goldman Sachs are described in Jensen and in Kenneth H. Bacon, "Penn Central Co. and Ex-Officers Are Charged..." *Wall Street Journal*, May 3, 1974, p. 3. (The statements on pages 22 and 23 of this book regarding actions of Goldman Sachs in the sale of Penn

Central commercial paper are in no way meant to imply or infer misuse of insider information.)

page 23 The amount of capital of Goldman Sachs at the time of Gus Levy's death is referred to in Garry Evans, "The Weinberg Interview," *Euromoney*, June 1990, p. 35.

CHAPTER 1 – Other References (i.e., works consulted by the author)

"The Biggest Bankruptcy Ever," *Time*, July 6, 1970, p. 58.

Vincent P. Carosso, *Investment Banking in America* (Cambridge, Mass.: Harvard University Press, 1970), pp. 18–20.

Rachel S. Epstein, *Investment Banking* (New York: Chelsea House, 1988), pp. 10 and 11–13.

Douglas Frantz, *Levine & Co.* (New York: Henry Holt, 1987), pp. 34–40.

Paul Hoffman, *The Dealmakers: Inside the World of Investment Banking* (Garden City, N.Y.: Doubleday, 1984), p. 48.

Kevin Lahart, "The Way We Were," *Financial World*, January 12, 1988, pp. 26–28.

Martin Mayer, *The Bankers* (New York: Weybright and Talley, 1974), pp. 51–52.

Barry E. Supple, "A Business Elite: German-Jewish Financiers in Nineteenth-Century New York," *Business History Review*, Summer 1957, pp. 147, 152, and 153.

"Uncle, Can You Spare Some Millions?" *Time*, June 22, 1970, p. 75.

J. Fred Weston and Eugene F. Brigham, *Managerial Finance* (Hinsdale, Ill.: The Dryden Press, 1978), pp. 463–464.

Jack Willoughby, "Can Goldman Stay on Top?" *Forbes*, September 18, 1989, pp. 150 and 154.

CHAPTER 2 – Notes

page 24 The figures stated for the reduction in stock commissions paid by institutional investors following May Day is based on data reported in Robert J. Cole, "Wall Street Notes Drop in Opposition to Rise in Big-Client Rates," *New York Times*, February 28, 1978, pp. 41 and 53.

pages 24–26 and 27 The changes in the investment-banking industry in the 1970s are the subject of Samuel L. Hayes III, "The Transformation of Investment Banking," *Harvard Business Review*, January-February 1979, pp. 153-170. The changes in the recruiting practices of investment-banking firms is described in Hayes, pp. 160–161. The changes in the background and knowledge of corporate financial managers is described in Hayes, pp. 155–156.

pages 26 and 27 The changes in underwriting resulting from Rule 415 are described in "The 1984 Corporate Sweepstakes," *Institutional Investor*, March 1984, p. 164, and in Tim Carrington, "Morgan Stanley, as Lead Manager, Led in Dollar Value of 1982 U.S. Underwritings," *Wall Street Journal*, January 11, 1983, p. 43.

page 27 First Boston's fee for advising Bendix in the Bendix/Martin Marietta affair is estimated as between $6 million and $8 million in Sandra Salmans, "Merger Advisers Under Fire: Wall Street Views Bendix Battle," *New York Times*, October 4, 1982, p. D1, and as $7 million in Tim Metz, "Goldman Sachs Avoids Bitter Takeover Fights but Leads in Mergers," *Wall Street Journal*, December 3, 1982, p. 1.

page 28 Goldman's policy regarding hostile bids is described in Tim Metz, "Goldman Sachs Avoids Bitter Takeover Fights but Leads in Mergers," *Wall Street Journal*, December 3, 1982, p. 18; in Anthony Bianco, "Parting Shots from Goldman Sachs' Whitehead," *Business Week*, November 12, 1984, p. 144; and in Jack Egan, "Nice Guys Finish First," *New York*, November 14, 1983, p. 14. Statements by Goldman leaders regarding the success of hostile bids are quoted by Metz and Bianco.

page 29 Goldman's underwriting ranking for corporate securities for 1983 is from rankings in "The 1984 Corporate Sweepstakes," *Institutional Investor*, March 1984, pp. 161 and 164.

page 29 The estimate for Goldman's pre-tax profit at the time of Gus Levy's death is based on the quote of Goldman Senior Partner and Chairman of the Management Committee (and son of Sidney Weinberg) John L. Weinberg in Garry Evans, "The Weinberg Interview," *Euromoney*, June 1990, p. 35, that profits had increased approximately 11 times since he became co-chairman (following the death of Gus Levy) and on figures in Michael Siconolfi, "Goldman Sachs Is Earnings King . . ." *Wall Street Journal*, September 21, 1992, p. C1, of pre-tax income of Goldman Sachs for each of its fiscal years 1987 through 1991 as reportedly stated in a confidential offering circular of private-placement notes of Goldman Sachs filed in September 1992, details of the offering circular originally being reported in Michael Liebowitz, "Goldman Raises $200 Million in Private Debt Market," *Investment Dealers' Digest*, September 21, 1992, pp. 5–6.

The $90 million figure for Goldman's capital at the time of Gus Levy's death is from a quote in Evans, p. 35.

page 29 Goldman Sachs' pre-tax profit for its fiscal 1983 is estimated as $400 million in Irwin Ross, "How Goldman Sachs Grew and Grew," *Fortune*, July 9, 1984, p. 156; in Scott McMurray, "Goldman Sachs's Whitehead to Resign, Leaving Weinberg as the Sole Chairman," *Wall Street Journal*, August 16, 1984, p. 31; and in Robert J. Cole, "Low-Profile Leader Takes Charge," *New York Times*, August 16, 1984, p. D5, and as between $350 and $400 million in Richard L. Stern, "A Money Machine," *Forbes*, January 2, 1984, p. 72.

page 30 The $432 million figure for the average level of partners' capital of Goldman for 1983 is a simple average of the beginning partners' capital of $363 million and the year-end amount of $502 million.

CHAPTER 2 – Other References

Karen W. Arenson, "How Wall Street Bred an Ivan Boesky," *New York Times*, November 23, 1986, Section III, p. 8.

Robert A. Bennett, "Can Mighty Goldman Stay Private?" *New York Times*, April 13, 1986, Section III, pp. 1 and 33.

Rachel S. Epstein, *Investment Banking* (New York: Chelsea House, 1988), pp. 14–15, 25–26, 34, and 36–37.

"ESB, in Switch, Decides to Back Inco's Tender Bid," *Wall Street Journal*, July 30, 1974, p. 3.

"ESB Urges Rejection of Inco Bid," *Wall Street Journal*, July 22, 1974, p. 18.

Garry Evans, "The Weinberg Interview," *Euromoney*, June 1990, p. 34.

Douglas Frantz, *Levine & Co.* (New York: Henry Holt, 1987), pp. 40–45.

John Koten and Virginia Inman, "Bendix to Pursue Martin Marietta with $1.5 Billion of Cash and Stock," *Wall Street Journal*, August 26, 1982, p. 2.

"The M&A Sweepstakes," *Institutional Investor*, February 1983, pp. 145–146.

Tim Metz, "Goldman Sachs Avoids Bitter Takeover Fights but Leads in Mergers," *Wall Street Journal*, December 3, 1982, p. 1.

Peter Petre, "Merger Fees that Bend the Mind," *Fortune*, January 20, 1986, p. 20.

Cary Reich, "Interview with John Whitehead," *Institutional Investor*, June 1987, pp. 28–29.

Irwin Ross, "How Goldman Sachs Grew and Grew," *Fortune*, July 9, 1984, pp. 156, 158, and 161.

Sandra Salmans, "Merger Advisers Under Fire: Wall Street Views Bendix Battle," *New York Times*, October 4, 1982, pp. D1 and D5.

Jack Willoughby, "Can Goldman Stay on Top?" *Forbes*, September 18, 1989, p. 158.

CHAPTER 3 – Notes

page 31 Drexel Burnham's underwriting status for 1983 is from rankings in "The 1984 Corporate Sweepstakes," *Institutional Investor*, March 1984, pp. 161 and 164.

page 31 Certain corporate investments of Carl Icahn during the period 1979 to 1983 are described in Connie Bruck, *The Predators' Ball* (New York: American Lawyer: Simon and Schuster, 1988), pp. 155–161.

pages 32 and 33 Kohlberg Kravis Roberts' bid for Gulf Oil is described in Allan Sloan, "Luring Banks Overboard?" *Forbes*, April 9, 1984, p. 40. The debt and preferred-stock securities in KKR's offer were of subjective value. Gulf Oil was acquired by Chevron (formerly Standard Oil of California) for $80 per share.

pages 33–35 The five-to-six-times cash flow rule of thumb for LBO pricing and much of the discussion of leveraged buyouts is based on the author's personal experiences in evaluating potential leveraged transactions for an industrial firm that he worked for in the 1980s.

pages 34–35 The origin of the term *mezzanine* financing and the use of such financing in leveraged buyouts is described in Allan Sloan, "Luring Banks Overboard?" *Forbes*, April 9, 1984, pp. 41 and 43.

pages 36–38 The Milken/Drexel financing system is explained in detail in Connie Bruck, *The Predators' Ball* (New York: American Lawyer: Simon and Schuster, 1988); the client relationship with First Investors Fund for Income is described in Bruck, pp. 33 and 46–47. The Milken/Drexel system is the subject of Allan Sloan and Howard Rudnitsky, "Taking In Each Other's Laundry," *Forbes*, November 19, 1984, pp. 207–222.

page 39 Union Oil's repurchase of shares from Daniel K. Ludwig is described in Frederick Rose, "Unocal's Chairman Speaks Out Against Forced Buybacks," *Wall Street Journal*, April 15, 1985, p. 19.

Notes and References 129

page 40 Fred Hartley's views on investment bankers are described in Frederick Rose, Laurie P. Cohen, and James B. Stewart, "How T. Boone Pickens Finally Met His Match: Unocal's Fred Hartley," *Wall Street Journal*, May 24, 1985, p. 16.

page 40 Besides Goldman Sachs, Unocal also used the firm of Dillon Read for advice in the Mesa Partners affair, as well as several law firms.

pages 42–43 Reasoning behind Unocal's exclusion of Mesa Partners from the 29 percent buyback is described in "Mesa Tells Court Barring by Unocal Violates Its Rights," *Wall Street Journal*, May 9, 1985, p. 8.

page 43 footnote The repurchases by Cities Service, Superior Oil, and Phillips Petroleum are described in Tim Metz and Doron P. Levin, "Cities Service Imposed Accord Ending Mesa Bid," *Wall Street Journal*, June 21, 1982, p. 2; Richard B. Schmitt, "Mesa to Sell Back 3% Stake It Holds in Superior Oil," *Wall Street Journal*, September 2, 1983, p. 4; and Charles F. McCoy, "Pickens Will Sell Phillips Holding Back to Company," *Wall Street Journal*, March 7, 1985, p. 10, respectively.

page 43 In July 1986, the SEC adopted the "all-holders rule," which prohibited companies from excluding shareholders from a tender offer in the manner that had been proposed by Unocal.

page 44 Goldman's fee for the Unocal repurchase is estimated in David Kirkpatrick, "Deals of the Year," *Fortune*, January 20, 1986, p. 27.

CHAPTER 3 – Other References

Edward I. Altman and Scott A. Nammacher, *Investing in Junk Bonds* (New York: John Wiley & Sons, 1987), pp. 46–47.

Michael Blumstein, "Phillips's Novel Defense Pact," *New York Times*, December 26, 1984, p. D5.

Connie Bruck, *The Predators' Ball* (New York: American Lawyer: Simon and Schuster, 1988), pp. 27, 66, 73–74, 107, 165–166, 167, and 176.

Bryan Burrough and John Helyar, *Barbarians at the Gate* (New York: Harper & Row, 1990), p. 140.

Michael Cieply, Earl C. Gottschalk Jr., and Laurie P. Cohen, "Unocal, in New Counter to Pickens, Seeks 29% of Its Shares for $72 Each in Notes," *Wall Street Journal*, April 24, 1985, p. 5.

Christopher Farrell, "LBOs: The Stars, the Strugglers, the Flops," *Business Week*, January 15, 1990, pp. 58 and 62.

David Kirkpatrick, "Deals of the Year," *Fortune*, January 20, 1986, pp. 27–29.

"A Leveraged Buyout: What It Takes," *Business Week*, July 18, 1983, pp. 194–195.

Charles F. McCoy, "Phillips Is Seen Possibly Exposed to a New Offer," *Wall Street Journal*, December 26, 1984, p. 3.

Charles F. McCoy, "Pickens Group Boosts Stake in Unocal to 13.6% with $322 Million Purchase," *Wall Street Journal*, March 28, 1985, p. 2.

Charles F. McCoy and Frederick Rose, "Pickens Group Details Two-Step Offer for Unocal Shares Totaling $8.1 Billion," *Wall Street Journal*, April 9, 1985, p. 2.

Charles F. McCoy and Frederick Rose, "Unocal Rejects Pickens Takeover Offer as Group Sets $3.9 Billion of Financing," *Wall Street Journal*, April 15, 1985, p. 2.

Charles F. McCoy, Rhonda L. Rundle, and Jennifer Bingham Hull, "Unocal Stake of 7.9% Bought by Pickens," *Wall Street Journal*, February 15, 1985, p. 3.

James R. Norman, "At Unocal, A Victory Without the Champagne," *Business Week*, June 3, 1985, p. 41.

Frederick Rose, Laurie P. Cohen, and James B. Stewart, "Unocal, Mesa Group Reach Pact to End Takeover Battle for Firm, *Wall Street Journal*, May 21, 1985, p. 2.

Frederick Rose, Laurie P. Cohen, and James B. Stewart, "How T. Boone Pickens Finally Met His Match: Unocal's Fred Hartley," *Wall Street Journal*, May 24, 1985, pp. 1 and 16.

Frederick Rose and Charles F. McCoy, "Unocal Sets Plan to Buy 49% of Its Stock in Effort to Thwart Takeover by Pickens," *Wall Street Journal*, April 17, 1985, p. 2.

Frederick Rose, Charles F. McCoy, and James B. Stewart, "Unocal Discloses Details of Stock Offer Aimed at Halting Takeover by Pickens," *Wall Street Journal*, April 18, 1985, pp. 2 and 16.

Barbara Rosewicz, "Avco Will Buy Its Shares Held by Leucadia," *Wall Street Journal*, August 30, 1984, p. 5.

Allan Sloan, "Luring Banks Overboard?" *Forbes*, April 9, 1984, pp. 40–41.

Benjamin J. Stein, "You Can Bank on It: Without Glass-Steagall, History Will Repeat," *Barron's*, February 4, 1991, pp. 16–17.

John D. Williams, "How 'Junk Financings' Aid Corporate Raiders in Hostile Acquisitions," *Wall Street Journal*, December 6, 1984, pp. 1 and 20.

CHAPTER 4 – Notes

page 46 John Kluge's background is described in "The Forbes 400," *Forbes*, October 27, 1986, p. 112.

page 46 The Prudential Insurance mezzanine funding in the Metromedia LBO was in the form of preferred stock, with warrants to purchase common stock. (Preferred stock, which is often used in leveraged-buyout financing, has characteristics of both debt and equity. In leveraged buyouts, it is often a type of mezzanine funding in that it does not participate in equity returns to the extent of common stock.) The financing for the Metromedia LBO also included debentures paid directly to the public stockholders as part of the purchase price for their shares.

page 46 The estimate of $2 billion of cash is the author's estimate based on the financing of the Metromedia LBO and the prices obtained for various properties sold off, and on figures reported in John Wilke, "Metromedia: Nothing Left but Money," *Business Week*, July 14, 1986, pp. 30–31.

page 46 The ranking of John Kluge's wealth is from "The Forbes 400," *Forbes*, October 27, 1986, p. 112.

pages 47–48 The LBO proposal regarding Macy's is described in R.H. Macy & Company, Proxy Statement for Special Meeting of Shareholders to Be Held on June 19, 1986. The events leading up to the board of directors' approval of the LBO are described in pages 10–16 of the Proxy Statement. The financing of the LBO is described in pages 14–16, 55–56, 60, and 64. The financial forecasts are stated on page 32. The estimated fees and expenses in connection with the LBO are stated on pages 53 and 54.

page 47 The four-times cash flow valuation is calculated as follows:

Operating Cash Flow Calculation

	$372 million	Earnings Before Income Taxes for Macy's fiscal year ended 8/3/85 (p. F-2 of Proxy Statement for Shareholder Meeting of 6/19/86)
add	$102 million	Net Interest Expense (p. F-2 of Proxy)
add	$103	Depreciation (p. F-5 of Proxy)
	$577 million	Operating Cash Flow (EBITD)

Market Valuation

	51.2 million	Average Number of Common Shares Outstanding during fiscal year ended 8/3/85 (p. 82 of Proxy)
mult. by	$45 a share	Market Price of Common Shares in spring 1985
	$2,304 million	Market Value of Common Shares
add	$134	Long-Term Debt (p. 82 of Proxy)
	$2,438 million	Market Value of Macy's Capitalization

	$2,438 million	Market Value
divide by	$577 million	Operating Cash Flow
	4.2	Multiple of Cash Flow

page 49 The housing-starts data are U.S. Department of Commerce figures as reported in *Industry Surveys*, February 21, 1991, p. B87.

pages 49–51 The LBO proposal regarding National Gypsum is described in National Gypsum Company, Proxy Statement/Prospectus for Shareholder Meeting of April 25, 1986. The events leading up to the board of directors' approval of the LBO are described in pages 29–32 of the Proxy. The discount debentures are described in pages 7–9, 29, 31, 52, and 61. The proposals made by Wickes Companies, the revised LBO proposals by the management group, and the responses by the special committee of National Gypsum's board of directors are described in pages 33–36.

page 49 The statement that National Gypsum's annual sales nearly doubled and its income more than tripled is based on financial data on page F-4 of the Proxy, showing net sales of $720 million and $1.34 billion for 1983 and 1985, respectively, and earnings from continuing operations (before extraordinary item) of $35.8 million and $116.1 million for 1983 and 1985, respectively.

page 49 The $9.50-per-share analysts' valuation estimate for the discount debentures is from Edwin A. Finn Jr. and Jonathan Dahl, "Bid for National Gypsum Valued at $1.1 Billion," *Wall Street Journal*, November 26, 1985, p. 3.

pages 49–50 The $11 per share of operating cash flow is calculated as follows:

Notes and References 133

	$222 million	Earnings Before Interest, Other Income, Income Taxes, and Extraordinary Item for National Gypsum fiscal year ended 12/31/85 (p. F-4 of Proxy Statement for Shareholder Meeting of 4/25/86)
add	$31	Depreciation (p. F-5 of Proxy)
	$253 million	Operating Cash Flow (EBITD)

	$253 million	Operating Cash Flow
divide by	22.8 million	Common Shares Outstanding at 12/31/85 (p. F-3 of Proxy) and to be purchased in LBO (p. 72)
	$11.10	Operating Cash Flow Per Share

Per page 100 of the Proxy, at 12/31/85 National Gypsum had cash and short-term investments of $68.3 million and long-term debt of $199.4 million.

page 51 The analysts' valuation estimate of "the low $60s" is from "Wickes Cos. Offers to Raise Bid to Buy National Gypsum," *Wall Street Journal*, April 18, 1986, p. 6.

page 51 The statement that the management-group offer was ostensibly worth at least $65 per share is based on the statements in the Proxy, page 35, that the proposal was intended to offer the National Gypsum stockholders consideration valued at $65 or more per share, plus the statement on page 52 of the Proxy that for certain purposes of valuing the consideration to be received from the proposal, National Gypsum assumed the initial market value of the debentures to be 50 percent of the face amount.

page 51 The financial projections for the National Gypsum LBO, including the projected capitalization, are summarized on page 58 of the Proxy. For the 1992 projections (the seventh year following the LBO), total long-term debt was projected as $1.382 billion (consisting of $1.015 billion of discount debentures, $350 million of subordinated debentures, and $17 million of other debt) and stockholders' equity was projected as $157.3 million at year's end. Earnings before interest and taxes (EBIT) for 1992 was projected as $219.5 million, and net interest expense was projected as $195.9 million. (The ratio of EBIT to net interest expense is commonly

134 *Notes and References*

referred to as the *interest coverage ratio*, a measure of a company's ability to meet its debt obligations.)

page 52   The statement regarding the increase in total debt of non-financial corporations is from Federal Reserve Board data as shown in a graph in Louis Uchitelle, "Pushing the Stakes to New Heights," *New York Times*, October 30, 1988, Section III, p. 1.

page 52   The events regarding Goldman's bond unit are described in Linda Sandler, "Goldman Is Being Aggressive in Bidding for Firms' Bonds," *Wall Street Journal*, January 9, 1985, p. 4, and in Matthew Winkler, "Goldman Hires Top Official of Salomon in Big Shake-Up of Debt Securities Area," *Wall Street Journal*, June 25, 1986, p. 26.

page 53   Goldman's volume relative to Salomon Brothers and Goldman's market share in public underwriting of mortgage-backed securities for 1986 is from data from IDD Information Services as reported in Ann Monroe, "Salomon Led U.S. Underwriting Ranks Again in 1986," *Wall Street Journal*, January 2, 1987, p. 17.

page 53   The revenue and profit figures of Drexel Burnham are from a financial statement released by the firm and reported in Steve Swartz, "Drexel Was Street's Most Profitable Firm in 1986, According to Its Financial Data," *Wall Street Journal*, May 8, 1987, p. 2.

CHAPTER 4 – Other References

Nigel Adam, "Goldman Travels Badly," *Euromoney*, June 1987, pp. 55–66.

Sarah Bartlett, "Look Who's Charging into the Merger Business," *Business Week*, March 9, 1987, p. 44.

Bryan Burrough and John Helyar, *Barbarians at the Gate* (New York: Harper & Row, 1990), pp. 207–208.

Laurie P. Cohen, "Macy's to Sell Some Interests to Westfield," *Wall Street Journal*, October 13, 1986, p. 2.

Christopher Farrell, "LBOs: The Stars, the Strugglers, the Flops," *Business Week*, January 15, 1990, pp. 58 and 62.

Edwin A. Finn Jr. and Jonathan Dahl, "Bid for National Gypsum Valued at $1.1 Billion," *Wall Street Journal*, November 26, 1985, p. 3.

Earl C. Gottschalk Jr., "Wickes Sells National Gypsum Stake," *Wall Street Journal*, April 28, 1986, p. 14.

Kathleen A. Hughes, "Wickes Launches Offer to Acquire National Gypsum," *Wall Street Journal*, April 11, 1986, p. 13.

Notes and References 135

Kathleen A. Hughes and Cynthia F. Mitchell, "Wickes Plans Tender Offer for Gypsum," *Wall Street Journal*, April 9, 1986, p. 2.

"Is Metromedia a Bargain at $1.5 Billion?" *Business Week*, December 19, 1983, pp. 31–32.

"Macy's Holders Clear $3.7 Billion Buyout of Retailing Concern," *Wall Street Journal*, June 20, 1986, p. 6.

"Prudential to Provide Loan of $800 Million," *Wall Street Journal*, May 15, 1986, p. 40.

Allan Sloan, "The Magician," *Forbes*, April 23, 1984, pp. 32–34.

Richard L. Stern and Edward F. Cone, "Scarlett O'Hara Comes to Wall Street," *Forbes*, September 21, 1987, pp. 37–38.

"Wickes Terminates $54-a-Share Offer for National Gypsum," *Wall Street Journal*, April 30, 1986, p. 42.

Jason Zweig and David Stix, "Tick, Tick, Tick," *Forbes*, August 6, 1990, p. 79.

CHAPTER 5 – Notes

page 58 The six-times cash flow valuation is calculated as follows:

Operating Cash Flow Calculation

	$80.8 million	Earnings Before Interest, Taxes, and Other Income/Expense for Multimedia for 1984
add	$21.5	Depreciation
	$102.3 million	Operating Cash Flow (EBITD)

Market Valuation

	16.7 million	Common Shares Outstanding
mult. by	$35 a share	Market Price of Common Shares in 12/84
	$584 million	Market Value of Common Shares
add	$73	Long-Term Debt at 12/31/84
subtract	$15	Cash and Marketable Securities at 12/31/84
	$642 million	Market Value of Multimedia Capitalization

	$642 million	Market Value
divide by	$102 million	Operating Cash Flow
	6.3	Multiple of Cash Flow

136 Notes and References

page 59 The $12.50 estimate for the value of the discount debentures is from a statement by a spokesman and member of the buyout group as reported in Jim Montgomery, "Multimedia Gets Buyout Proposal of $825 Million," *Wall Street Journal*, February 4, 1985, p. 11.

page 60 The approximately $13 estimate for the value of the discount debentures was the high end of a range estimated by the management-led group as reported in Scott Kilman, "Multimedia Inc. Approves Offer of $890 Million," *Wall Street Journal*, April 9, 1985, p. 7.

page 60 A characterization by Multimedia of the new plan as a recapitalization was reported in Scott Kilman, "Multimedia Inc. Approves Offer of $890 Million," *Wall Street Journal*, April 9, 1985, p. 7.

pages 61–62 The "not for sale" response in regard to the Lorimar offer was reported in Jim Montgomery, "Multimedia Inc. Rejects Second Takeover Bid," *Wall Street Journal*, April 12, 1985, p. 4.

page 62 Cooke's second proposed offer was for a price of "more than $65" per share.

page 65 One of the FMC employee-benefit plans, the Stock Fund of the Thrift and Stock Purchase Plan, would have each share it currently held exchanged for four new shares and $25 cash (later revised to 4.209 shares and $25 cash).

page 65 Certain aspects of share rollovers and rollover ratios in recaps that are stated here are from the author's experience in analyzing recap transactions and participating in the enactment of a leveraged recapitalization. Also, the term *rollover* as used in regard to the conversion of shares in a recap came into general use later. In documents filed with the SEC in regard to the FMC recap, the conversion of shares was termed an "exchange."

pages 72–73 The Owens-Corning recap proposal is described in Owens-Corning Fiberglas Corporation, Proxy Statement/Prospectus for Special Meeting of Stockholders to Be Held on November 5, 1986. Wickes Companies' actions and other events prior to the board of directors' approval of the recap are described on pages 25 and 26 of the Proxy. An implied price range of $15.30 to $17.90 (per share) for the discount debentures based on prevailing yields of similar securities appears on page 31. The estimate of the stub-share value appears on page 30. The actions of Wickes Companies following the board of directors' approval of the recap plan are stated on page 26.

page 73 Analyst valuation estimates of $14 to $17 per share for the discount debentures are cited in Jerome Zukosky, Dan Cook, and Stewart

Troy, "Owens Corning Saves Itself—With a Scorched-Earth Strategy," *Business Week*, September 15, 1986, p. 49.

CHAPTER 5 – Other References

Jeff Bailey, "FMC Doesn't Plan Sale of More Assets for Restructuring," *Wall Street Journal*, May 6, 1986, p. 47.

Anthony Bianco and Teresa Carson, "A Takeover Target Trying to Be Its Own White Knight," *Business Week*, April 14, 1986, p. 39.

Michael Blumstein, "Phillips's Novel Defense Pact," *New York Times*, December 26, 1984, pp. D1 and D5.

"Colt Says Financing for Recapitalization Has Been Arranged," *Wall Street Journal*, September 8, 1986, p. 36.

"Cooke Makes Peace with Multimedia," *Business Week*, August 5, 1985, p. 38.

Geraldine Fabrikant, "Cooke Sells Stake to Multimedia," *New York Times*, July 20, 1985, pp. 31 and 33.

FMC Corporation, Form S-4 and Proxy Statement/Prospectus filed with Securities and Exchange Commission on May 2, 1986.

"FMC Corp. Plans Recapitalization," *Journal of Commerce*, February 25, 1988, p. 21B.

Nick Gilbert, "Stacking the Deck," *Financial World*, June 2, 1987, p. 42.

Hank Gilman, "Colt Industries Offers Proposal to Recapitalize," *Wall Street Journal*, July 21, 1986, p. 2.

Pamela G. Hollie, "Lorimar in Bid for Multimedia," *New York Times*, April 11, 1985, p. D5.

Robert Johnson and Marj Charlier, "FMC Clears Plan to Shrink Sharply Public Ownership," *Wall Street Journal*, February 24, 1986, p. 49.

Scott Kilman, "Multimedia Inc. Approves Offer of $890 Million," *Wall Street Journal*, April 9, 1985, p. 7.

The Kroger Company, Letter to Shareholders, November 21, 1988, pp. 4–6.

Gene C. Marcial, "Boesky's Big Gamble at FMC," *Business Week*, April 28, 1986, p. 82.

Jim Montgomery, "Multimedia Gets Buyout Proposal of $825 Million," *Wall Street Journal*, February 4, 1985, p. 11.

Jim Montgomery, "Cooke Tells Multimedia He Would Lift Offer for Firm to at Least $1.08 Billion," *Wall Street Journal*, May 13, 1985, p. 10.

138 *Notes and References*

Christopher Power, "One Year Later, Colt Is at a Steady Gallop," *Business Week*, October 19, 1987, p. 134.

Allan Sloan, "The Magician," *Forbes*, April 23, 1984, p. 34.

Randall Smith, "Colt Industries Uses Novel Recapitalization that Sharply Boosts Debt to Lift Stock Price," *Wall Street Journal*, July 24, 1986, p. 53.

Timothy K. Smith, "Multimedia Bid Raised by Cooke to $70.01 a Share," *Wall Street Journal*, July 16, 1985, p. 14.

Robert Willens, "Are Recaps Tax Friendly to Stockholders?" *Mergers & Acquisitions*, March/April 1988, p. 46.

CHAPTER 6 – Notes

page 75 The four-times cash flow valuation is calculated as follows:

Operating Cash Flow Calculation

	$38.6 million	Operating Income Before Income Taxes for Warnaco Inc. for 1985
add	$8.9	Interest Expense
add	$7.2	Depreciation
	$54.7 million	Operating Cash Flow (EBITD)

Market Valuation

	10.2 million	Average Number of Common Shares Outstanding in 1985
mult. by	$21 a share	Market Price of Common Shares in early 1985
	$214 million	Market Value of Common Shares
add	$30	Long-Term Debt in 1985
subtract	$14	Cash and Short-Term Investments
	$230 million	Market Value of Warnaco Capitalization

	$230 million	Market Value
divide by	$54.7 million	Operating Cash Flow
	4.2	Multiple of Cash Flow

page 76 The estimated valuation of the discount debentures at $6 per share, and the LBO proposal at $33 per share, is based on a $33.30-per-share valuation of a final, slightly revised LBO proposal, such figure being reported in Daniel Hertzberg, "Warnaco's Resistance to Hostile Tender Offer Is Evoking Cynicism Among Some Analysts," *Wall Street Journal*, April 3, 1986, p. 51, and in Earl C. Gottschalk Jr. and Daniel Hertzberg, "Warnaco Clears $46.50-a-Share Offer by Group," *Wall Street Journal*, April 28, 1986, p. 4, and on the highest trading price for Warnaco shares (of $32.50) between the announcement of the original LBO proposal and board approval of the revised plan.

pages 76–78 The LBO proposal for Warnaco and the initial proposed recap plan are described in Warnaco Inc., Proxy Statement/Prospectus for Shareholder Meeting of April 25, 1986. Events leading up to the board of directors' approval of the LBO proposal are described in pages 25–27 of the Proxy. Events from the time of the approval of the LBO plan until a Warnaco board meeting to review the revised W Acquisition tender offer of $40 per share are described in pages 27–29. The financing of the original recap plan is described in pages 43, 47, 59, and 68–69.

page 77 The statement that the original Warnaco recap distribution was expected to be worth more than $36 per share is based on Warnaco's management presenting the plan to the board of directors as an alternative that would be, in management's opinion, financially superior to W Acquisition's $36-per-share tender offer, such presentation being described on page 28 of the Proxy, and on the statement on page 59 of the Proxy that the $29-per-share face value of notes and debentures in the distribution were anticipated to trade at their stated face amounts.

page 79 The figure for fees in the Beatrice LBO (and subsequent refinancings and divestitures) is the author's estimate based on figures reported in John D. Williams, "Kohlberg Kravis to Get $45 Million Fee if Its Purchase of Beatrice Is Completed," *Wall Street Journal*, March 19, 1986, p. 5; in Daniel P. Wiener, "Deals of the Year," *Fortune*, February 2, 1987, p. 69; and in Laura Jereski, "Me Too, Me Too," *Forbes*, September 21, 1987, p. 38.

page 79 The figure for Drexel's fees is from Laura Jereski, "Me Too, Me Too," *Forbes*, September 21, 1987, p. 38.

page 79 The statements regarding equity warrants and the value of equity holdings are based on data in Laura Jereski, "Me Too, Me Too," *Forbes*, September 21, 1987, p. 38; in Connie Bruck, *The Predators' Ball* (New York: American Lawyer: Simon and Schuster, 1988), p. 250; and in

James B. Stewart, *Den of Thieves* (New York: Simon and Schuster, 1991), p. 192.

page 81 After a concern was expressed by the Federal Reserve Board regarding whether the agreement, as proposed, between Goldman and Sumitomo Bank met the provisions of the Bank Holding Company Act of 1956, the agreement was revised to limit Sumitomo Bank's investment to 24.9 percent of Goldman's equity capital, and the initial investment reportedly was less than $500 million.

page 81 The quote by John L. Weinberg, who was Chairman of Goldman's Management Committee and Senior Partner, appeared in Steve Swartz and George Anders, "Goldman Sachs Weighs Selling Stake in Profits," *Wall Street Journal*, August 7, 1986, p. 3, and in James Sterngold, "Sumitomo of Japan Plans to Buy a Stake in Goldman Sachs," *New York Times*, August 7, 1986, pp. A1 and D4.

page 82 The statements regarding Goldman's use of Japanese sources to purchase subordinated debt from leveraged deals is based in part on the author's experience in the financing of a recapitalization advised on by Goldman Sachs.

CHAPTER 6 – Other References

Nigel Adam, "Goldman Travels Badly," *Euromoney*, June 1987, p. 66.

"Another Diver in the Buy-Out Pool," *The Economist*, April 15, 1989, p. 82.

Robert A. Bennett, "Can Mighty Goldman Stay Private?" *New York Times*, April 13, 1986, Section III, p. 33.

Anthony Bianco and Teresa Carson, "A Takeover Target Trying to Be Its Own White Knight," *Business Week*, April 14, 1986, pp. 38–39.

Meg Cox, "Warnaco Raises Recapitalization Offer to Stymie Suitor," *Wall Street Journal*, April 9, 1986, p. 10.

Christopher Farrell, "King Henry," *Business Week*, November 14, 1988, p. 127.

Earl C. Gottschalk Jr. and Daniel Hertzberg, "Warnaco Clears $46.50-a-Share Offer by Group," *Wall Street Journal*, April 28, 1986, p. 4.

"Group Sweetens Bid for Warnaco to $44 a Share," *Wall Street Journal*, April 14, 1986, p. 18.

Roy J. Harris Jr., "Warnaco Gets $367.2 Million All-Cash Offer," *Wall Street Journal*, March 18, 1986, p. 10.

Diana Henriques, "Yen to Grow: Goldman Sachs's New Japanese Connection," *Barron's*, August 11, 1986, p. 26.

Notes and References 141

Jed Horowitz, "Citicorp Investment Fund Poised for Mezzanine Deals," *American Banker*, July 26, 1989, p. 15.

John Marcom Jr., "Warnaco Inc. Proposes Recapitalization to Block $367.2 Million Takeover Bid," *Wall Street Journal*, March 25, 1986, p. 10.

Frederic A. Miller and Amy Borrus, "How Megadebt Shakes Up Banks and Bonds," *Business Week*, November 14, 1988, p. 132.

Nathaniel C. Nash, "Goldman's Japan Tie Is Cleared," *New York Times*, November 20, 1986, pp. D1 and D9.

Michael Quint, "Expanding Role of Junk Bonds," *New York Times*, November 17, 1988, p. D5.

Kevin Rafferty, "Probing the Sumitomo Culture," *Institutional Investor*, November 1986, p. 296.

"Sobering Up," *The Economist*, October 21, 1989, p. 91.

James Sterngold, "Sumitomo of Japan Plans to Buy a Stake in Goldman Sachs," *New York Times*, August 7, 1986, pp. A1 and D4.

James Sterngold, "Wall Street Deals: Ante Is Raised," *New York Times*, November 6, 1986, p. D10.

James Sterngold, "Deep-Pocketed Deal Makers," *New York Times*, April 14, 1987, pp. D1 and D8.

Steve Swartz and George Anders, "Goldman Sachs Weighs Selling Stake in Profits," *Wall Street Journal*, August 7, 1986, p. 3.

"Warnaco Suitor Is Prepared to Pay Over $425 Million," *Wall Street Journal*, April 8, 1986, p. 20.

Daniel P. Wiener, "Deals of the Year," *Fortune*, February 2, 1987, p. 71.

John E. Yang, "Fed Approves Goldman Stake for Sumitomo," *Wall Street Journal*, November 20, 1986, pp. 3 and 21.

CHAPTER 7 – Notes

page 83 The statements that the dollar volume of M&A transactions reached a record level in the fourth quarter of 1986 and returned to the average 1986 pace in the second quarter of 1987 is based on data on dollar volume of total merger & acquisition activity as reported in "Quarterly Profile," *Mergers & Acquisitions*, March/April 1987, p. 71 and March/April 1988, p. 70.

page 83 The investigation of Drexel by the SEC was reported in Daniel Hertzberg and James B. Stewart, "SEC Is Probing Drexel on 'Junk

Bonds,' Ties to Boesky," *Wall Street Journal*, November 18, 1986, pp. 3 and 24.

page 86   The Household International poison pill and the events surrounding its enactment are the subject of "A 'Poison Pill' That's Super-Lethal," *Business Week*, October 1, 1984, pp. 93–94.

page 87   The term *Big Three* as applied to Citicorp, Manufacturers Hanover, and Bankers Trust in regard to leveraged-deal lending is mentioned in Bryan Burrough and John Helyar, *Barbarians at the Gate* (New York: Harper & Row, 1990), pp. 207–208. The syndication and sale of leveraged-deal bank loans and bank fees from such lending are described in Sarah Bartlett, "Need a Quick Billion or Two? Just Ask Your Banker," *Business Week*, October 26, 1987, pp. 98–99.

pages 89–90   Merchant banking, bridge loans, and bridge-loan fees are the subject of James Sterngold, "Deep-Pocketed Deal Makers," *New York Times*, April 14, 1987, pp. D1 and D8.

page 91   The Jerome S. Kohlberg Jr. quote appeared in "The Forbes 400," *Forbes*, October 24, 1988, p. 242.

page 92   Exchange offers and Drexel's use of such offers are the subject of Dierdre Fanning, "Spoilsport Lawyers," *Forbes*, December 1, 1986, pp. 209–210, and are described in Connie Bruck, *The Predators' Ball* (New York: American Lawyer: Simon and Schuster, 1988), pp. 75–77.

page 93   The quote by John L. Weinberg appeared in "Wall Street's Shining Maiden," *The Economist*, September 29, 1990, p. 93. Also, in Garry Evans, "The Weinberg Interview," *Euromoney*, June 1990, p. 34, Weinberg is quoted as saying, "When it's all your own money and you have unlimited liability, you watch the eggs very carefully and you try to take only sensible risks."

CHAPTER 7 – Other References

Harry Berkowitz, "The Kravis Appetite for High Stakes Deals," *Newsday*, April 3, 1988, p. 54.

Connie Bruck, *The Predators' Ball* (New York: American Lawyer: Simon and Schuster, 1988), p. 250.

Wendy Cooper, "An Ineffective Poison Pill," *Institutional Investor*, January 1984, p. 256.

Cynthia Crossen, "Merger Activity Expected to Ease, not Halt," *Wall Street Journal*, January 2, 1987, p. 8B.

Peter L. Faber and Arthur H. Rosenbloom, "Living with the New Tax Law: M&A Under the New Rules," *Merger Management Report*, Cambridge Corporation, 1987, pp. 2-5.

Udayan Gupta, "Wesray and Chairman Simon Cancel Start-Up of Leveraged Buyout Fund," *Wall Street Journal*, January 30, 1986, p. 5.

Sally Saville Hodge, "Chicago's Unabashed Centimillionaire," *Forbes*, May 30, 1988, p. 254.

Carol J. Loomis, "LBOs Are Taking Their Lumps," *Fortune*, December 7, 1987, pp. 63 and 64–65.

Carol J. Loomis, "The Biggest Looniest Deal Ever," *Fortune*, June 18, 1990, pp. 51 and 54.

Frederic A. Miller and Amy Borrus, "How Megadebt Shakes Up Banks and Bonds," *Business Week*, November 14, 1988, p. 132.

National Gypsum Company, Proxy Statement/Prospectus for Shareholder Meeting of April 25, 1986, pp. 31 and 74.

Stephen Phillips, "Revco: Anatomy of an LBO that Failed," *Business Week*, October 3, 1988, p. 58.

Michael Quint, "Southland Proposal to Finance Buyout," *New York Times*, December 2, 1987, pp. D1 and D7.

Michael Quint, "Expanding Role of Junk Bonds," *New York Times*, November 17, 1988, pp. D1 and D5.

William E. Sheeline, "Deals of the Year," *Fortune*, February 1, 1988, p. 37.

Pamela Sherrid, "Making the Best Deals Their Own," *U.S. News & World Report*, June 30, 1986, p. 47.

Michael Siconolfi, "Salomon Will Pay Nearly $30 Million in Revco Settlement," *Wall Street Journal*, October 31, 1991, p. C20.

Randall Smith and Ann Monroe, "Insider-Trading Jitters Deal Another Setback to Junk-Bond Market," *Wall Street Journal*, November 20, 1986, pp. 1 and 20.

"Southland Buy-Out Financing Revised by Goldman Sachs," *Wall Street Journal*, November 9, 1987, p. 37.

James Sterngold, "Wall St. Deals: Ante Is Raised," *New York Times*, November 6, 1986, p. D10.

James B. Stewart and Daniel Hertzberg, "Investment Bankers Feed a Merger Boom and Pick Up Fat Fees," *Wall Street Journal*, April 2, 1986, p. 16.

Lois Therrien, "Beatrice Investors Will Just Have to Sit Tight," *Business Week*, March 12, 1990, p. 104.

144 *Notes and References*

Joseph Weber and Christopher Farrell, "A Junk-Bond Belly Flop," *Business Week*, November 23, 1987, p. 35.

Robert Willens, "Are Recaps Tax Friendly to Stockholders?" *Mergers & Acquisitions*, March/April 1988, p. 46.

Matthew Winkler, "Goldman Shakes Up Fixed-Income Unit," *Wall Street Journal*, July 15, 1988, p. 18.

Jerome Zukosky, "Nobody Can Do a Deal Quite Like Wesray," *Business Week*, September 1, 1986, p. 29.

CHAPTER 8 – Notes

page 94 The $3.8 billion value for the LBO of Montgomery Ward includes $2.3 billion of debt assumed by the purchaser.

page 95 The $30 million fee for Goldman was reported in Ronald Henkoff, "Deals of the Year," *Fortune*, January 30, 1989, p. 163.

page 96 The four-times cash flow valuation is calculated as follows:

Operating Cash Flow Calculation

	$323 million	Earnings Before Income Taxes for Kroger for the year ended 1/2/88
add	$96	Interest Expense (net of interest income)
	$419 million	Earnings Before Interest and Taxes (EBIT)
add	$223	Depreciation
add	$237	Rent Expense*
	$879 million	Operating Cash Flow (EBITD)**

Market Valuation

	78.6 million	Common Shares Outstanding
mult. by	$34 a share	Market Price of Common Shares in summer 1985
	$2,672 million	Market Value of Common Shares
add	$780	Long-Term Debt at 6/18/88
add	$195	Obligations Under Capital Leases* at 6/18/88
subtract	$142	Cash and Temporary Cash Investments at 6/18/88
	$3,505 million	Market Value of Kroger Capitalization

Notes and References   145

	$3,505 million	Market Value
divide by	$879 million	Operating Cash Flow
	4.0	Multiple of Cash Flow

* Many of Kroger's facilities were rented, and such rentals were, in effect, a significant form of long-term financing for the company. Rental expense is therefore added back to income (in the manner of interest expense) to arrive at a pre-financing-expense cash flow, and capital lease obligations are included in the capitalization figure as a type of long-term debt obligation.

** Kroger's EBITD for the period 1/3/88 to 6/18/88 was $441 million, or an annualized amount of approximately $960 million.

page 96 Dart Group's and the Herbert Haft family's purchases of stakes of, offers for, and requests for antitrust clearance regarding companies prior to Kroger are detailed in Bryan Burrough, "Kroger Gets Haft Family Proposal with Indicated $4.36 Billion Value," *Wall Street Journal*, September 20, 1988, p. 3.

page 96 The fifth case of an action by Dart Group prior to an LBO was the purchase of a stake in Jack Eckerd Corporation.

page 97 The stub and total-recap value estimates are based on analyst estimates of $5 to $7 for the stub and $53 to $55 per share for the recap package as reported in Carol Hymowitz, "Kroger Unveils Tentative Plan to Restructure," *Wall Street Journal*, September 14, 1988, p. 3.

pages 97–100 The Kroger recapitalization plan and the events surrounding it are described in The Kroger Company, Letter to Shareholders, November 21, 1988. In the Shareholder Letter, the plan is referred to as a "Restructuring Program."

page 98 The valuation estimate for the stub shares is described on page 4 of the Shareholder Letter.

page 98 The proposals contained in the letter from KKR are described on pages 4–5 of the Shareholder Letter.

pages 98–99 The basis of the Kroger board's September 23 approval of the recap plan is described on pages 3–4 of the Shareholder Letter.

page 99 The initial financing required for the recapitalization was $4.88 billion, consisting of $3.234 billion of bank loans, $1.0 billion of subordinated notes, and $647 million of discount debentures to be distributed to the shareholders, such financing being described on page 7 of the Shareholder Letter. The total bank-lending commitments were $3.6 billion, which included additional amounts in a working-capital credit facility and a divestiture-loan commitment, such commitments being described on page 30 of the Shareholder letter.

pages 99–101 Statements regarding certain facets of the Kroger recapitalization are based in part on the author's discussions with Goldman Sachs personnel regarding the Kroger recap.

pages 99–100 The events of the October 7 Kroger board meeting and the basis of the board's conclusion regarding KKR's proposals and the recap plan are described in pages 5–6 of the Shareholder Letter.

page 100 Shortly before the recap dividend was to be paid, it was disclosed that a KKR affiliate had accumulated a 9.9 percent holding in Kroger's common shares "solely for the purpose of investment." No further proposals were made by KKR, and soon thereafter it was announced that KKR planned to dispose of the investment.

page 100 The issuance of the $1 billion of subordinated debt in connection with the payment of the cash portion of the Kroger dividend is described on pages 8 and 32 of the Shareholder Letter.

page 100 The statement regarding total subordinated-debt financing fees is based on a $15 million fee for the initial placement of the subordinated debt, as shown under estimated transaction costs on page 7 of the Shareholder Letter, and on a $43.75 million fee for a public offering of $1.25 billion of debentures on January 19, 1989, as reported in Christopher Knowlton, "Deals of the Year," *Fortune*, January 29, 1990, p. 142 and in Matthew Winkler, "Poor Results in 1989 May Show Profit Erosion for Junk Bonds," *Wall Street Journal*, January 2, 1990, p. R26. The $25 million advisory-fee figure is the Investment Banker Management Fee stated on page 7 of the Shareholder Letter and reported in Ronald Henkoff, "Deals of the Year," *Fortune*, January 30, 1989, p. 163.

page 102 The M&A ranking referred to is from Securities Data Corporation as reported in Randall Smith and David B. Hilder, "Takeover Drought Parches Dealmakers," *Wall Street Journal*, January 2, 1990, p. C1.

CHAPTER 8 – Other References

Bryan Burrough, "Kroger Gets Haft Family Proposal with Indicated $4.36 Billion Value," *Wall Street Journal*, September 20, 1988, p. 3.

Bryan Burrough, "KKR Makes an Unsolicited Offer for Kroger Totaling $4.64 Billion," *Wall Street Journal*, September 21, 1988, p. 3.

Bryan Burrough and John Helyar, *Barbarians at the Gate* (New York: Harper & Row, 1990), pp. 305–307, and 372–374.

Robert J. Cole, "Kraft Rejects Bid of Philip Morris; Offers $14 Billion Dividend Plan," *New York Times,* October 24, 1988, pp. A1 and D3.

Kurt Eichenwald, "Kraft Takeover: Swift and Smooth," *New York Times*, November 3, 1988, p. D2.

Patricia Gallagher, "Takeover Attempt Long Expected by Analysts," *Cincinnati Enquirer*, November 6, 1988.

Ronald Henkoff, "Deals of the Year," *Fortune*, January 30, 1989, pp. 162–163.

Carol Hymowitz, "Kroger Unveils Tentative Plan to Restructure," *Wall Street Journal*, September 14, 1988, p. 3.

Christopher Knowlton, "Deals of the Year," *Fortune*, January 29, 1990, p. 137.

Carol J. Loomis, "The Biggest Looniest Deal Ever," *Fortune*, June 18, 1990, pp. 62 and 68.

Frederic A. Miller and Amy Borrus, "How Megadebt Shakes Up Banks and Bonds," *Business Week*, November 14, 1988, p. 132.

Floyd Norris, "The Trader," *Barron's*, September 19, 1988, p. 71.

Floyd Norris, "Kraft Plan Pares Margin for Error," *New York Times*, October 26, 1988, p. D10.

"Quarterly Profile," *Mergers & Acquisitions*, March/April 1988, p. 70.

"Quarterly Profile," *Mergers & Acquisitions*, March/April 1989, p. 74.

Matthew Schifrin, "Where's the Buyer?" *Forbes*, September 19, 1988, p. 218.

William E. Sheeline, "Kroger in the Ring," *Fortune*, October 24, 1988, p. 16.

Randall Smith, "Merger Boom Defies Expectations," *Wall Street Journal*, January 3, 1989, p. 8R.

James Sterngold, "Forstmann Declines to Bid on RJR Nabisco," *New York Times*, November 17, 1988, pp. D1 and D15.

Gregory Stricharchuk, "Kroger Rejects Offers, Intends to Restructure," *Wall Street Journal*, September 26, 1988, p. 4.

Gregory Stricharchuk, "Kroger Chief Expects Asset Sale to Reap $333 Million for Bid to Stay Independent," *Wall Street Journal*, September 27, 1988, p. 7.

Gregory Stricharchuk, "KKR Ends Bid to Buy Kroger, Avoiding Fight," *Wall Street Journal*, October 12, 1988, p. A3.

"Trashing Wall Street's Golden Years," *The Economist*, January 27, 1990, p. 79.

Ralph E. Winter and Gregory Stricharchuk, "Kroger Rejects KKR Bid, Sticks to a Revamping," *Wall Street Journal*, October 10, 1988, p. A5.

CHAPTER 9 – Notes

page 103   The Air Line Pilots Association was acting as representative of the United Air Lines pilots.

pages 103–105   The buyout proposal for UAL Corporation is described in Airline Acquisition Corporation, Schedule 14D-1, September 25, 1989. The financing for the buyout is described in the Transaction Overview section. The financial projections and underlying assumptions are described on page 57.

page 105   The figures for the Buyout Group Projection of UAL Operating Profit included in the graph consist of the Operating Income line shown on page 57 of Airline Acquisition Corporation, Schedule 14D-1 dated 9/25/89, and in Project Sky King, Base Case, Historical and Projected Income Statements in Airline Acquisition Corporation, Schedule 14D-1 dated 10/2/89, plus the ESOP Contribution line in Schedule 14D-1 dated 10/2/89. The ESOP Contribution expense is added back here because the ESOP (Employee Stock Ownership Plan) was to be used as a form of financing in the buyout. For the 1989 operating-income figure, the pro forma annual labor savings of $265 million shown in the projection in Schedule 14D-1 dated 10/2/89 was removed, as such savings would have been minimal from the time of the completion of the buyout to the end of 1989.

page 105   The statement that the UAL buyout group's projections had double-digit percentage growth in revenues is based on the Total Revenues line in Project Sky King, Base Case, Historical and Projected Income Statements in Airline Acquisition Corporation, Schedule 14D-1 dated 10/2/89, and in page 57 of Schedule 14D-1 dated 9/25/89. The statement regarding growth in operating profit is based on the operating-profit figures in the graph on text page 106, which are described in the preceding note. The statement regarding growth in cash flow is based on the EBDIAT (Earnings Before Depreciation, Interest, Amortization, and Taxes) line in Schedule 14D-1 dated 10/2/89, with the figure for 1989 having the pro forma annual labor savings of $265 million removed, as such savings would have been minimal from the time of the completion of the buyout to the end of 1989.

page 106 The commercial banks' October 13, 1989 rejection of participation in the UAL buyout financing is the subject of Jeff Bailey, Asra Q. Nomani, and Judith Valente, "Banks Rejecting UAL Saw Unique Defects in This Buy-Out Deal," *Wall Street Journal*, October 16, 1989, pp. A1 and A6.

pages 106–107 The events in stock trading on October 13, 1989 are described in Randall Smith, "Stock Market Braces for a Crucial Test After Friday's Plunge," *Wall Street Journal*, October 16, 1989, pp. A1 and A6.

page 107 The Donald Trump quote appeared in "What's News," *Wall Street Journal*, October 17, 1989, p. A1.

pages 108–112 The factors in the downfall of Drexel Burnham are described in Judith H. Dobrzynski, Leah J. Nathans, John Meehan, and Eric Shine, "After Drexel," *Business Week*, February 26, 1990, pp. 37–40, and in Chris Welles, "So Long, Sorcery. Hello, Sanity," *Business Week*, February 26, 1990, p. 42.

page 109 Key aspects of the junk-bond market are described in Constance Mitchell, "Hourly Price Quotes on Some Junk Bonds Planned in Bid to Curb Unruly Trading," *Wall Street Journal*, November 11, 1992, pp. C1 and C11.

pages 110–111 The default rate stated for junk bonds for 1989 is based on information in Constance Mitchell, "Junk-Bond Defaults Expected to Multiply," *Wall Street Journal*, January 2, 1991, p. R6, and in Gary Hector, "Junk's Bad Times Are Just Starting," *Fortune*, June 4, 1990, p. 82. The figure stated for 1990 is based on information in Constance Mitchell, "Junk-Bond Defaults Expected to Multiply," *Wall Street Journal*, January 2, 1991, p. R6.

page 111 The figure for HLT loans is based on data in Gary Hector, "Junk's Bad Times Are Just Starting," *Fortune*, June 4, 1990, p. 82.

page 111 The statement regarding M&A dollar volume is based on figures reported in "Quarterly Profile," *Mergers & Acquisitions*, March/April 1990, p. 125 and March/April 1991, p. 103, and in "Decade in Review," *Mergers & Acquisitions*, March/April 1990, p. 95.

page 111 The statement regarding junk-bond underwriting volume is based on data from IDD Information Services as reported in Kurt Eichenwald, "Offerings Set a Record, but Fees Slip," *New York Times*, January 2, 1991, p. D14. The statement regarding fees for junk-bond underwriting are based on data from Securities Data Company as reported in Michael Siconolfi, "Wall Street's Fees Fall to Six-Year Lows," *Wall Street Journal*, January 2, 1991, p. R21.

page 111 The "more than $200 million" amount is based on figures stated in James B. Stewart, *Den of Thieves* (New York: Simon & Schuster, 1991), p. 410, and in Bryan Burrough and John Helyar, *Barbarians at the Gate* (New York: Harper & Row, 1990), p. 510.

CHAPTER 9 – Other References

Connie Bruck, *The Predators' Ball* (New York: American Lawyer: Simon and Schuster, 1988), p. 77.

John J. Curran, "Hard Lessons from the Decade of Debt," *Fortune*, June 18, 1990, p. 77.

Kurt Eichenwald, "Junk Bond Staff Cut by Drexel," *New York Times*, November 15, 1989, p. D5.

James E. Ellis, "United's Buyers May Be Wearing Rose-Colored Goggles," *Business Week*, October 16, 1989, p. 36.

James E. Ellis, "This Is Too Big a Genie to Put Back in the Bottle," *Business Week*, November 6, 1989, p. 43.

Debbie Galant, "Crossing the Line," *Institutional Investor*, July 1991, pp. 119–120.

Carole Gould, "When Bonds Act Like Stocks," *New York Times*, April 21, 1991, Section III, p. 13.

Gary Hector, "Junk's Bad Times Are Just Starting," *Fortune*, June 4, 1990, pp. 81, 82, and 88.

David B. Hilder and Linda Sandler, "Mega-Merger Game Will Survive, Some Say, but Tone Will Change," *Wall Street Journal*, October 16, 1989, p. C2.

"Hostile M&A Market Conditions Block the Intended Sales of Many Good Companies," *National Review of Corporate Acquisitions*, August 27, 1990, p. 1.

Susan E. Kuhn, "Junk: The Weak and the Strong," *Fortune*, October 23, 1989, p. 17.

James P. Miller, "Pepperell Group Is Suing Farley Over Takeover," *Wall Street Journal*, March 19, 1992, p. A4.

Constance Mitchell, "Junk-Bond Defaults Expected to Multiply," *Wall Street Journal*, January 2, 1991, p. R6.

Linda Sandler, Randall Smith, and Joan Lebow, "How Junk Bonds Came to Rescue, Then Strangled Integrated," *Wall Street Journal*, June 23, 1989, p. A9.

"Shaken and Stirred," *The Economist*, October 21, 1989, p. 92.

Michael Siconolfi, "Wall Street's Fees Fall to Six-Year Lows," *Wall Street Journal*, January 2, 1991, p. R21.

Randall Smith, "Rash of Corporate Sell-Offs Undercutting Asset Values," *Wall Street Journal*, November 7, 1990, pp. C1 and C15.

James B. Stewart, *Den of Thieves* (New York: Simon & Schuster, 1991), pp. 427 and 432.

"Trashing Wall Street's Golden Years," *The Economist*, January 27, 1990, pp. 79–80.

UAL Corporation, Annual Report for 1989, pp. 10–11.

"Wall Street Journal Starts New Feature on 'Junk' Bonds," *Wall Street Journal*, January 3, 1991, p. C14.

"What a Difference a Year Makes: A Peek Backward to the M&A Market of the Fall of 1989," *National Review of Corporate Acquisitions*, September 10, 1990, p. 1.

Matthew Winkler, "Poor Results in 1989 May Show Profit Erosion for Junk Bonds," *Wall Street Journal*, January 2, 1990, p. R26.

Matthew Winkler, "Underwriting Profits Skidded in 1989," *Wall Street Journal*, January 2, 1990, p. R26.

Matthew Winkler and Constance Mitchell, "Trading in Junk Bonds Collapses, While Treasurys Stage Big Rally," *Wall Street Journal*, October 16, 1989, p. C1.

CHAPTER 10 – Notes

pages 115–116 The statements regarding the record level of underwriting activity and Goldman's rank in domestic underwriting volume, equity underwriting, and junk-bond underwriting are based on data from Securities Data Company as reported in William Power, "Stock-and-Bond Issuance Exploded in 1991," and Michael Siconolfi, "Underwriting Fees End Their Four-Year Tailspin," *Wall Street Journal*, January 2, 1992, p. R32, and Michael Siconolfi, "Junk Bonds Set Sail for Modest Recovery," *Wall Street Journal*, January 2, 1992, p. R6.

page 117 The statement regarding Goldman's position in M&A is based in part on rankings for total dollar volume of transactions completed as compiled by Securities Data Company and reported in Randall Smith, "Wall Street's Longtime Stars Lead the Dealmakers' League," *Wall Street Journal*, January 2, 1991, p. C1.

page 117 In its 1990 Annual Review, page 12, Goldman Sachs states that it represented both Avery International Corporation and Dennison Manufacturing Company in their merger.

152 Notes and References

page 119 The Shearson Lehman bridge loan, which was for an LBO of Prime Computer, was settled for cash and an equity interest in Computervision Corporation (a successor of Prime Computer Inc.), which did a securities offering in 1992.

page 119 The class-action lawsuit by Revco securities holders referred to here was settled in 1991, as described in Michael Siconolfi, "Salomon Will Pay Nearly $30 Million in Revco Settlement," *Wall Street Journal*, October 31, 1991, p. C20.

page 119 The figure of 50,000 persons losing their jobs in the securities industry is from Eva Pomice and Dana Hawkins, "Will Wall Street Ever Coin Money Again?" *U.S. News & World Report*, January 21, 1991, p. 64.

page 120 The pre-tax profit of Goldman Sachs for its 1991 fiscal year reportedly was stated in a confidential offering circular of private-placement notes of Goldman Sachs filed in September 1992, as reported in Michael Siconolfi, "Goldman Sachs Is Earnings King on Wall Street, With Record 1991 Pretax Profit of $1.15 Billion," *Wall Street Journal*, September 22, 1992, p. C1, and in Adam Bryant, "Glimpse of Goldman Sachs: Pretax Profit of $1.15 Billion," *New York Times*, September 22, 1992, pp. D1 and D19, details of the Goldman offering circular originally being reported in Michael Liebowitz, "Goldman Raises $200 Million in Private Debt Market," *Investment Dealers' Digest*, September 21, 1992, pp. 5–6.

CHAPTER 10 – Other References

George Anders, "Duracell International Plans to Go Public in Offering to Raise Up to $280 Million," *Wall Street Journal*, March 20, 1991, p. A6.

George Anders, "Stop & Shop to Offer Shares for $250 Million," *Wall Street Journal*, October 10, 1991, p. A4.

George Anders, "More 1980s LBOs Rush to Go Public Again," *Wall Street Journal*, January 21, 1992, p. C1.

Sarah Bartlett, "Need a Quick Billion or Two? Just Ask Your Banker," *Business Week*, October 26, 1987, pp. 98–99.

Fred R. Bleakley, "A Decade of Debt Is Now Giving Way to the Age of Equity," *Wall Street Journal*, December 16, 1991, pp. A1 and A8.

Anne Newman, "Debt-Paring Fuels Surge in Initial Stock Offerings," *Wall Street Journal*, January 2, 1992, p. R3.

Frederic A. Miller and Amy Borrus, "How Megadebt Shakes Up Banks and Bonds," *Business Week*, November 14, 1988, pp. 132–133.

Eva Pomice and Dana Hawkins, "Will Wall Street Ever Coin Money Again?" *U.S. News & World Report*, January 21, 1991, pp. 64–65.

William Power, "Wall Street Racks Up an Underwriting Record," *Wall Street Journal*, October 1, 1991, p. C19.

Michael Siconolfi, "First Boston to Sell 'Bridges' to Its Owners," *Wall Street Journal*, November 6, 1990, pp. C1 and C11.

Michael Siconolfi, "Junk Bonds Set Sail for Modest Recovery," *Wall Street Journal*, January 2, 1992, p. R6.

Michael Siconolfi, "Underwriting Fees End Their Four-Year Tailspin," *Wall Street Journal*, January 2, 1992, p. R32.

Leah Nathans Spiro, Blanca Riemer, and Richard A. Melcher, "The Inside Battle Is About Over at First Boston," *Business Week*, February 18, 1991, pp. 110–111.

Leah Nathans Spiro and John Templeman, "A Short Leash for First Boston," *Business Week*, November 26, 1990, p. 156.

"Trashing Wall Street's Golden Years," *The Economist*, January 27, 1990, pp. 79–80.

Chris Welles and John N. Frank, "Did Drexel Bully Takeover Candidates?" *Business Week*, March 9, 1987, p. 43.

John R. Wilke and Randall Smith, "Computervision's Shares Plummet 35% on Bleak 3rd-Quarter Profit Forecast," *Wall Street Journal*, October 1, 1992, p. A4.

Index

acquisition-depreciation tax shield, 90–91
Air Line Pilots Association, 103
Allied Stores, 80, 89
American Airlines *See* AMR Corporation
American National Resources, 36, 38
American Standard, 101
AMR Corporation, 106–107
arbitrage *See also* takeover-stock arbitrage
  in "break-up" deals, 85
  defined, 22
Avco Corporation, 36

Bankers Trust, 46, 87, 87*n*
banks, commercial *See* commercial banks; *specific banks*
B.A.T. Industries/Farmers Insurance Group merger, 94
Beatrice LBO, 48, 79, 85, 96
Bendix vs. Martin Marietta *See* mergers and acquisitions
Bloomingdale's, 110, 111
Boesky, Ivan, 66, 83, 90, 110
Borg-Warner LBO, 88, 89
"break-up" deals, 84–85, 91
"bridge" financing/loans, 80–81, 89–90, 92–93, 106
  described, 80–81
  "double fees" in, 80–81, 89
  refinancing of, 80, 81, 89, 90, 92–93, 102, 108, 119
British Airways, 103
Burlington Industries LBO, 88

Campeau Corporation, 80, 89, 94, 102, 110, 111, 119
cash flow
  importance in LBOs, 33–34
  multiple, defined, 47*n*
  multiples, 84, 91
  operating, defined, 34*n*
Castle & Cooke, 101
Chase Manhattan Bank, 20, 105
Citibank, 47, 47*n*, 89
Citicorp, 46, 47*n*, 87, 87*n*, 105

Clayton & Dubilier, 36
Coastal Corporation, 36
Colt Industries, 73–74
Columbia Savings and Loan, 36
commercial banks
  in 1920s leverage system, 18–19
  and leveraged-deal lending, 32, 35, 47, 53, 84–85, 87–88, 98, 99, 111, 118
  "Big Three" bank lenders, 87, 95, 101
  "due diligence" work in, 88, 118
  fees from, 35, 79, 88, 118
  "highly leveraged transaction" (HLT) loan portfolios, 111
  loan syndicates, 87, 118
  in UAL buyout plan, 103–107
  and securities underwriting, 20, 53
commercial paper, 15, 21, 109, 112
  and Penn Central bankruptcy, 22–23
Connecticut General/INA merger, 28, 29*n*
Cooke, Jack Kent, 62–63
corporate executives
  1980s fears, 38, 45
"cram-down" debt, 44
  defined, 32–33
  use in mezzanine financing, 32–33, 49–50, 51, 77, 78

Dart Group, 96–98
Del Monte, 102
Walt Disney Productions, 36
Drexel Burnham, 9, 31, 32, 36–38, 52, 58, 61, 74, 81, 90, 91–92, 93
  and Beatrice LBO, 79
  downfall of, 102, 107–112
  fees in leveraged deals, 36, 79, 90, 112
  financing speed of, 35, 36, 40, 76
  "highly confident" letter of, 38–39, 50, 76, 108
  and mezzanine financing, 35, 48, 79
  profits of, 53
  and RJR Nabisco LBO, 95, 101, 111
  SEC investigation of, 83, 90, 102

EBITD *See* cash flow, operating

Farley, William, 36, 108
Farmers Insurance Group *See* B.A.T. Industries/Farmers Insurance merger
Federal Communications Commission (FCC), 59
Federated Department Stores, 94, 102, 110
financial leverage *See* leverage
financial securities *See* securities
Finkelstein, Edward, 47
First Boston, 31*n*, 61, 90, 92, 119
  creation of, 20
  and bridge financing, 80, 81, 89, 92, 102, 119
First Executive, 37
First Investors Fund for Income, 36
First National Bank of Boston, 20
FMC Corporation, 64–67
Ford Motor Company, 29
Forstmann Little, 101
Fort Howard LBO, 94
Fruehauf LBO, 88

Galef, Andrew, 76
General Electric, 29, 119
General Electric (GE) Credit, 48, 76
Gibson Greetings LBO, 33, 34
Glass-Steagall Act, 20
Goldman, Henry, 16
Goldman, Marcus, 15
Goldman Sachs, 53, 102, 119
  1920s mutual-fund/underwriting/leverage system, 17–19, 37
  1980s success of, 10, 11, 117–118, 120
  bond operations, 52
  and bridge financing, 81, 92–93
  capital of, 23, 29, 29*n*, 82, 120
  and commercial paper, 15–16, 21, 29, 53
  early history of, 15–20
  and equity underwriting, 16, 52, 116
  fees from leveraged deals, 44, 48, 67, 100
  Japanese financing contacts, 81–82
  junk-bond-financing abilities of, 52, 92, 116
  and Kraft defense, 95
  and Kroger recap, 97–101
  and mergers and acquisitions (M&A), 22, 27–29, 117
  as advisor to both sides in a merger, 28–29, 117
  as defender of corporations, 38, 39, 101
  nonhostile policy, 28, 117
  ranking, 29, 102, 117
  mezzanine-financing abilities of, 41, 48–49, 52, 78, 81–82, 99, 100
  and mortgage-backed securities, 53
  and Multimedia, 59–64
  partners of, 11, 30
  and Penn Central, 22–23, 28
  profits of, 11, 29–30, 120
  return on equity, 30
  and RJR Nabisco, 101–102
  and securities underwriting, 16–20, 21, 27, 31*n*, 116
  and Southland LBO financing, 92–93
  as trusted firm, 21, 28, 40, 117
  underwriting rank, 29, 116
  Unocal defense, 40–44
  and Warnaco, 75–78
Goldman Sachs Trading Corporation, 18–19, 37
Grand Metropolitan/Pillsbury merger, 94
greenmail, 31
  defined, 31*n*
  reversal of in Unocal defense, 42–43
Gulf Oil/Chevron merger, 32, 95

Haft, Herbert, 96–97
Harcourt Brace Jovanovich (HBJ), 92
Harte-Hanks Communications, 58
Hartley, Fred, 39–44
Hart-Scott-Rodino (HSR) filing, 96
Holiday Corporation, 92
hostile offer, 38–39
  defined, 26*n*
Household International, 86
housing starts, 49

Icahn, Carl, 31, 36
INA Corporation, 28, 29*n*
Inco/ESB merger *See* mergers and acquisitions
institutional investors
  as junk-bond purchasers, 90
  as LBO financiers and investors, 35, 41, 48

insurance companies, 36, 87
  in 1920s leverage system, 18–19
  as junk-bond purchasers, 36–37
  as mezzanine financiers, 35
Integrated Resources, 109
investment banking *See also specific topics such as* securities underwriting
  1930s changes in, 20
  1970s changes in, 24–27
  effect of "May Day" on, 24–25
  hierarchy of underwriting, 20–21
  and securities underwriting, 16
  separation from commercial banks, 20, 53
investment-grade debt, 31n, 36, 109n

Japanese investors, 82
junk bonds/securities, 9, 10, 31, 37, 38, 79, 81, 83, 90, 92–93, 102, 116
  in Beatrice LBO, 79
  collapse of market in, 106, 107–112
  defaults, 92, 107, 110–111
  defined, 31n
  fees from, 36, 90, 111
  in Gulf Oil bid, 32
  in leveraged deals, 35–36
  market, described, 109–110
  in mezzanine financing, 35, 79, 103

Kidder Peabody, 119
KKR (Kohlberg Kravis Roberts), 36, 91, 96, 116
  Beatrice LBO, 79
  Gulf Oil bid, 32
  Kroger proposal, 97–100
  RJR Nabisco LBO, 95, 101–102
Kluge, John, 33, 45–46
Kohlberg, Jerome, 91
Kraft, 94, 95
Kroger, 96–101
Kuhn, Abraham, 15

Lazard Freres, 29n
Lehman Brothers, 17, 29n
Lenox, Inc., 86n
Leucadia National, 36
leverage, 9, 19
  crazes/eras, 9, 10, 17–18, 119
  downfall of 1980s era, 102, 106–112, 119

defined, 33n
leveraged buyouts (LBOs), 41, 45, 46, 47, 68–69, 71–72, 85, 89, 90, 111
  described, 33–35
  equity returns from, 33n, 34, 46, 79
  fees from, 48, 79
  financing structure of, 33n, 33–35, 51, 103
  management role in, 71
  pricing multiple of, 34
  sale of equity in, 34, 116
  surplus/hidden assets and, 34, 47
leveraged deals
  bank syndicates in, 87–88
  divestitures from, 33, 34, 46, 79, 81, 84–85, 89, 101–102, 108, 111
  loan fees, 35, 88, 89–90
  projections/forecasts in, 51, 71, 85, 88, 103–105
  tax-law changes and, 83–84, 91
leveraged recapitalization *See* recap
Levy, Gustave (Gus), 22, 23, 29, 120
Loeb, Solomon, 15
Lorimar, 61–62
Ludwig, Daniel, 39

Macy's (R.H. Macy & Company) LBO, 47–48, 76
Manufacturers Hanover, 46, 47, 87, 87n
Martin Marietta vs. Bendix *See* mergers & acquisitions
May, Peter, 36
"merchant banking" strategy, 88–89, 119
mergers and acquisitions (M&A), 10, 22, 26, 27, 81, 83, 85–86, 111, 117
  1986 tax-law changes and, 83–84
  and Bendix/Martin Marietta/Allied Corporation affair, 26–27, 28
  effect of Inco/ESB merger on, 26
  "Pac-Man" bid/defense, 26
Merrill Lynch, 25, 31n, 80, 81, 89, 90, 96, 119
Mesa Partners II, 39–43
Mesa Petroleum, 32 *See also* Pickens, T. Boone Jr.
Metromedia LBO, 33, 45–46, 85
mezzanine financing, 58, 78n, 81, 82, 89, 103
  and bridge loans, 80–81, 89–90
  definition, 34–35
  in leveraged buyouts, 34–35, 46

158 Index

Milken, Michael, 9, 31, 36, 48, 52, 102
   use of equity warrants, 38, 79
   and Gulf Oil bid, 32
   junk-bond system of, 9, 36–38, 40, 79
   market-supporting tactics of, 91–92, 107, 108
   separation from Drexel, 102, 107
   and unregistered exchange offers, 92
"mirror" transactions, 91
Montgomery Ward LBO, 94
Morgan, J.P., 29
(J.P.) Morgan Bank, 20
Morgan Stanley, 20, 25, 31n, 61, 73, 80, 81, 89, 90
mortgage-backed securities, 53
Morton-Norwich/Thiokol Corporation merger, 28–29, 29n
Multimedia, 58–64
mutual funds, 18, 36–37, 87

National Can, 36
National Gypsum LBO, 49–52
Northwest Industries, 36, 38

Occidental Petroleum/Cities Service merger, 29
Owens-Corning, 72–73, 77
Owens-Illinois LBO, 89, 116

Panic of 1907, 17
Pantry Pride, 36
Peltz, Nelson, 36
Penn Central, 22–23, 28
pension-plan asset recapture, 91
Perelman, Ronald, 36
Philip Morris, 94, 95
Phillips Petroleum, 39, 43n, 61, 73
Pickens, T. Boone Jr.
   Gulf Oil bid, 32
   vs. Phillips Petroleum, 39, 43n
   vs. Unocal, 39–43
poison pills, 57, 86–87
Procter & Gamble, 29, 101
Prudential Insurance, 46
"Public LBO" *See* recap

Ralston Purina, 101
recap (recapitalization)
   advantage over LBO, 68–69, 71–72
   advantage over outside bids, 68–71, 99–101
   defense aspects of, 63–64, 65, 67–72, 75, 78, 99–101
   fees from, 58, 64, 67, 100
   FMC plan, 64–65
   Kroger plan, 97–101
   management returns in, 58, 64, 71–72
   Multimedia plan, 60–62
   "not a sale" aspect of, 61–62, 64, 68–69, 99, 100
   Owens-Corning plan, 73
   rollover of shares in, 65–66, 73
   shareholder vote in, 69, 100
   stockholder returns from, 63, 64, 66–67, 69–71
   stub-share valuation in, 70
   tax aspects of, 65
   tender offer versus, 101n
   value comparison versus outside bid, 69–71, 77–78, 98–100
   value edge/wildcard, 57, 61
   Warnaco defeat, 77–78
Revco Drug Stores, 91, 110
"reverse" LBOs, 116
Revlon, 36
R.J. Reynolds/Heublein merger, 29
RJR Nabisco, 94, 95, 101–102, 111, 116
Rosenwald, Julius, 15–16
Rule 415 *See* shelf registration

Sachs, Samuel, 16
Safeway Stores, 96, 116
Salomon Brothers, 25, 29n, 31n, 81, 95, 119
   and mortgage-backed securities, 53
   in Southland LBO, 92–93
Santa Fe Southern Pacific Corporation, 101
savings and loans (S&Ls), 36, 37, 87, 111
Sears Roebuck, 29
   initial equity offering of, 17
securities, publicy traded, 17, 17n
Securities and Exchange Commission (SEC), 17n, 18, 26, 83, 102
securities underwriting, 115
   1930s changes, 20
   description of, 16
   effect of 1979 IBM offering on, 25–26
   effect of shelf registration on, 26
   hierarchy of, 20–21, 118
   and syndication, 17, 87
Seligman, Joseph, 15

Shearson Lehman, 80, 81, 90, 95, 101, 119
shelf registration (of securities), 26, 27
"short swing" rule, 42n
Sigoloff, Sanford
   and National Gypsum bid, 50–51
   and Owens-Corning bid, 72
Simon, William, 91
   and Gibson Greetings LBO, 33
   and Multimedia recap, 59, 59n
Southland Corporation LBO, 92–93
Steinberg, Saul, 36
stock buybacks, 38, 41–44
stock-market crash of 1929, 19
stock-market crash of 1987, 92, 94, 107
Stop & Shop, 96, 116
Storer Communications, 36, 58
"stub" shares, 69–71, 73, 77, 95, 97, 98
Sumitomo Bank, 81
Supermarkets General, 88, 96

takeover-stock arbitrage, 22, 27, 40, 42, 106–107
   description of, 22
tender offer, hostile
   definition, 26n
Trump, Donald, 106, 107

TWA, 36
"two step" tender offer, 62, 86–87
   described 39–40

UAL Corporation, 103–107, 110
underwriting *See* securities underwriting
Uniroyal, 36
United Airlines *See* UAL Corporation
Unocal, 39–44
USG Corporation, 101
U.S. Steel/Marathon Oil merger, 29

WA Acquisition, 76–78
Wachtell Lipton, 60
Wall Street Journal, 38
Warnaco, 75–78
Wasserstein Perella, 102
Weinberg, John, 81, 93
Weinberg, Sidney, 20, 21, 22, 23, 120
Wesray, 59, 59n
West Point-Pepperell, 108
"white knight"
   definition, 32n
Wickes Companies, 50–51, 72–73 *See also* Sigoloff, Sanford
Wometco Enterprises, 58